LEEDS UNITED
PLAYER BY PLAYER

ANDREW MOURANT

GUINNESS PUBLISHING

ACKNOWLEDGEMENTS

In preparing this book, I should like especially to thank Ivan Ponting for his help and friendship, and Julian Barker for his research and vigilance. I am also indebted to Steve Small, Andy Cowie at Colorsport, Graham Hart, Eddie Gray, Bobby Collins, Jimmy Lumsden, Syd Owen, Peter Gunby, Jenny and Michael Thompson, Ian Smith, Colin Jeffrey, and the Yorkshire Evening Post picture library.

The author is also grateful for permission to reproduce photographs.
The vast majority are from Colorsport, who never cease to amaze with their ability to come up with a picture of just about anybody who has ever kicked a ball. Further contributions from the Yorkshire Evening Post, and Julian Barker.

Efforts have been made to trace copyright holders of all photographs used in this book.
We apologise for any omissions, which are unintentional, and would be pleased to include appropriate acknowledgement in any subsequent edition.

Pictured on the front cover are: *(clockwise from top left)* Johnny Giles, Don Revie, Billy Bremner, Gordon Strachan, Jack Charlton and Rod Wallace.

On the back are: *(centre)* Lee Chapman, *(clockwise from top left)* Norman Hunter, Paul Reaney, Tony Currie, Eddie Gray, David Batty and Allan Clarke.

First published in 1992 by
GUINNESS PUBLISHING
33 London Road, Enfield
Middlesex, EN2 6DJ

This book is a product of
FORSTER books

Designed by Steve Small

Text copyright © 1992 by Andrew Mourant

Illustrations copyright © 1992 as credited

A catalogue record for this book is available
from the British Library

Printed and bound in Great Britain by The Bath Press.

'Guinness' is a registered trademark
of Guinness Publishing Ltd

ISBN: 0-85112-568-9

INTRODUCTION

The years since 1961 have largely eclipsed Leeds United's earlier history. Don Revie's transition from wise senior player to manager brought about a revolution at Elland Road. In less than ten years, he created, from a mouldering debt-ridden football club that had won nothing apart from the second division, one to rank among Europe's finest. There can have been fewer more decisive appointments in soccer management and so it is with the coming of Revie that Leeds United-*Player by Player* begins.

There were, of course, other excellent players and sound teams in the more distant past. John Charles was an indomitable figure in the 1950s and it is fortuitous he returned briefly to Leeds under Revie's management so that his record, with photograph, can be included here along with that of every other player to pull on a Leeds United shirt since March 15 1961, the day the Revie era began.

The aim is to capture the flavour of each player, though where his contribution has been minimal, I have recorded only his career statistics. All records, including service with other clubs, are complete to the end of the 1991/2 season. The numerical information covers games played (substitute appearances in brackets are not included in the first figure), goals scored, international caps won and previous clubs. Leeds United appearance and scoring figures refer to all matches in the Football League, FA Cup, League Cup and European competitions but exclude other tournaments. (A breakdown for each competition may be found at the end of the book.) Under the heading of 'Other Clubs' however, the games and goals refer to Football League matches only. The dates in large type refer to the seasons in which each player appeared in the Leeds first team and not when he joined or left the club. Similarly under 'Other Clubs', dates relate to first team appearances. Honours include only those won as a Leeds United player except in relation to international caps. Transfer fees, where mentioned, are those reported in the press.

Leeds United-*Player by Player* is ushered in with a pictorial record of some of the stars of earlier eras and Raich Carter's team of the 1950s which won promotion from the second division and held considerable promise. Few would have predicted its rapid demise followed by the startling emergence of Revie's rasping team that matured to such greatness. Now, after many desperate empty seasons, the Leeds United playing story ends on a high note: the Howard Wilkinson era, in which pride has been restored and the club is back where it belongs, among the heavyweights and as First Division Champions.

Andrew Mourant,
Bradford on Avon,
May 1992.

CONTENTS

LEEDS UNITED 1956/7

Back row *(left to right):*

ERIC KERFOOT (49/50-58/9, wing-half, 349 games, 10 goals).

JIMMY DUNN (47/8-58/9, left-back, 443 games, 1 goal).

ROY WOOD (53/4-59/60, goalkeeper, 203 games, 0 goals).

ARCHIE GIBSON (54/5-59/60, right-half, 174 games, 5 goals).

GRENVILLE HAIR (50/1-63/4, left-back, 474 games, 2 goals).

Front row:

JACK CHARLTON (52/3-72/3, centre-half, 772 games, 95 goals).

GEORGE MEEK (52/3-59/60, winger, 199 games, 19 goals).

JOHN CHARLES (48/9-56/7, & 62/3, centre-half/centre-forward, 327 games, 157 goals).

HAROLD BROOK (54/5-57/8, forward, 106 games, 47 goals).

JACK OVERFIELD (55/6-59/60, left-wing, 163 games, 20 goals).

BOBBY FORREST (52/3-58/9, inside-forward, 121 games, 37 goals).

That there were sound Leeds United teams capable of exciting, even exhilarating football before the eras of Don Revie and Howard Wilkinson is often overlooked. Yet the class of 1929/30, managed by Dick Ray, finished fifth in the first division, scoring 79 goals.

The half-back line of Willis Edwards, Ernie Hart and George Reed, combining muscularity and passing skill, was the backbone of a fine side which had as its spearhead Tom Jennings, who, with 112 goals was Leeds top scorer before John Charles, and inside-left Russell Wainscoat, both of whom plundered defences in the late 1920s.

But next season came relegation; an assured-looking team was suddenly uncertain and the defence easy meat away from home. Inconsistency always plagued Leeds and thus it was when, nearly 30 years later, the astute Raich Carter brought Leeds out of the second division then lifted them to eighth in the league in 1956/7 before relegation followed three years later.

Carter was unlucky. He was forced to part with the irrepressible Charles - who scored 38 of Leeds 72 league goals - yet was given less than half the £65,000 to spend on new talent. The class of 1956 had about it a solid, dependable air: five players, Wood, Dunn, Hair, Kerfoot and Overfield were ever-present; Gibson, Meek and Charles missed only two league games each. But, Charles apart, only Jack Charlton among them lasted to sample future glories.

RAICH CARTER

JOHN CHARLES

TOMMY BURDEN

WILLIS EDWARDS

TOM JENNINGS

TOM HOLLEY

TOMMY BURDEN (48/9-54/5, wing-half, 259 games, 13 goals).

WILLIS EDWARDS (24/5-38/9, right-half, 444 games, 6 goals).

TOM JENNINGS (24/5-30/1, centre-forward, 174 games, 117 goals).

TOM HOLLEY (36/7-48/9, centre-half, 169 games, 1 goal).

GEORGE MILBURN (28/9-36/7, right-back, 166 games, 1 goal).

JIM MILBURN (39/40-51/2, full-back, 220 games, 17 goals).

ERNIE HART (20/1-35/6, centre-half, 472 games, 15 goals).

JACK MILBURN (29/30-39/40, left-back, 408 games, 30 goals).

BERT SPROSTON (33/4-37/8, right-back, 140 games, 1 goal).

ALBERT NIGHTINGALE (52/3-56/7, inside-forward, 135 games, 48 goals).

JACK MARSDEN (52/3-58/9, centre-half, 75 games, 0 goals).

JOHN SCOTT (50/1-54/5, goalkeeper, 114 games, 0 goals).

HARRY SEARSON (49/50-51/2, goalkeeper, 116 games, 0 goals).

GEORGE MILBURN

ERNIE HART

JIM MILBURN

JACK MILBURN

BERT SPROSTON

HAROLD WILLIAMS

ALBERT NIGHTINGALE

JACK MARSDEN

JOHN SCOTT

HARRY SEARSON

HUGH BAIRD

TED BURGIN

CHRIS CROWE

JIMMY ASHALL

TED BURGIN (58/9-60/1, goalkeeper, 59 games, 0 goals).

HUGH BAIRD (57/8-58/9, centre-forward, 45 games, 22 goals).

HAROLD WILLIAMS (49/50-55/6, winger, 229 games, 35 goals).

JOHN SCOTT (49/50-54/5, goalkeeper, 114 games, 0 goals).

CHRIS CROWE (56/7-59/60, winger, 98 games, 27 goals).

JIMMY ASHALL (55/6-60/1, full-back. 91 games, 0 goals).

JOHN CHARLES

It is almost a soccer cliche to prefix any mention of John Charles with the words "The Legendary". Even in Don Revie's great teams he would have been outstanding; pre-dating them, as he did, he appeared a colossus and a miracle of versatility.

Although brought up in the Welsh valleys, where rugby was a surrogate religion, from his childhood days Charles was set on a soccer career. Fame would come as a prolific scorer at centre-forward but it was at full-back that Charles played in the Swansea schools' team. Yet to his local league team, Swansea Town, John Charles did not appear to have any talent separating him from dozens of other young hopefuls.

Leeds United's scouts in South Wales thought otherwise. On the strength of their reports, United manager Major Frank Buckley brought Charles to Elland Road. As the Major surveyed his new recruit, almost six feet tall and rock solid, he felt Charles had the potential to be a defensive lynchpin at centre-half. It was there that Charles, aged 17 and four months, made his debut against Blackburn Rovers at Ewood Park in April 1949 with United toiling in the lower reaches of division two.

Events moved rapidly for the prodigious young footballer who became known as the Gentle Giant. By March 1950, less than a year after he entered senior football, Charles had made his international debut for Wales against Northern Ireland. Although he was tried occasionally at centre-forward, the conversion proper did not begin until 1952/3. Goals started to come by the bucketful; 26 that season, in which Charles still managed to help out the defence in his old slot, then 42 from 39 league matches during 1953/4 in performances which showed an awesome combination of power and control.

At number 5, number 9 or, for good measure at number 8, Charles' contribution played a crucial part as, in the 1955/6 season Leeds finally emerged from the obscurity of division two. The game at Hull City on April 28 1956 that clinched promotion typified the potent Charles effect; goals from a booming left foot shot early in the match then a second half penalty smashed in with all Charles' beef helped set up a 4-1 win.

In the end, John Charles outgrew the unfashionable club he had served so well. He hungered for football at the highest level and by May 1957, manager Raich Carter was unable to convince him Leeds United could satisfy his ambitions. Leaving behind thousands of distraught supporters, Charles departed to Juventus for a world record £65,000 and made hay among some of Europe's meanest club defences - he won three Italian Championship medals and was voted Italy's footballer of the year - before Don Revie brought him back to Leeds in August 1962 for £53,000.

It was not, however, a glorious home-coming. Charles, now 30, had little appetite for being cast in the role of Messiah, nor for the grind of division two football and Les Cocker's arduous training sessions. In eleven games he scored just three goals before departing to Roma for £65,000. In the end, nothing was lost and vivid memories of John Charles' greatness shone untarnished by a lingering decline and fall.

BORN: Swansea 27.12.31.
GAMES: 327. GOALS: 157.
HONOURS: 38 Wales Caps 50-65.
OTHER CLUBS: Juventus, Italy 57/8-61/2;
Roma, Italy 62/3; Cardiff City 63/4-64/5 (66, 19).

1948/49 - 1956/57 & 1962/63

GRENVILLE HAIR

Grenville Hair was a durable consistent figure in a succession of Leeds United teams that endured fluctuating fortunes during the 13 years he played first team football. Though an accomplished defender, who played latterly at right-back as well as his favoured position on the left, Hair was a full-back of the old school and another era; a player of undemonstrative efficiency who rarely had rushes of blood to the head egging him forward as an auxiliary midfielder or winger in search of goal-scoring glory. He scored just once in 443 league appearances.

Born in Burton-on-Trent, Hair had become a local athletics champion before Major Frank Buckley spotted him playing local football in 1948. It was more than two years before he broke into the Leeds United first team but by the 1951/2 season, aged just 20, he had made the left back position his own.

It is argued Hair might have played for England, rather than just take part in FA touring teams to the West Indies, Africa and New Zealand, had he been with a more fashionable club. While many things around him were falling apart, Hair was a great source of comfort to successive Leeds United managers; a player they knew would give a good solid performance. While not the fastest or the tallest defender, with experience Hair acquired two of the most valuable assets for a top class full back: composure and anticipation. And he could be a touch ruthless when the situation demanded it.

Yet he didn't lack style: from the neatness of his passing to the smartness of his appearance; and from what sometimes appeared a dour exterior came flashes of humour. Hair's career at Leeds lasted until 1964 when he left to become player-manager of Wellington Town (who later became known as Telford United). He suffered an untimely death in March 1968, aged only 36, when as manager of Bradford City, he had a heart attack after supervising training.

BORN: Burton on Trent, 16.11.31.
GAMES: 474. GOALS: 2.
MANAGER: Bradford City 67/8.

1950/51 - 1963/64

JOHN McCOLE

John McCole managed to thrive despite the declining Leeds team around him. He was brought to Elland Road from Bradford City in September 1959 but his 45 league goals in just 78 appearances coincided with his club's darkest days; relegation from the top flight and the ignominious possibility of the third division.

The robust Scotsman was not the tallest centre-forward - just five feet ten and a half - yet was good in the air. Through bravery and skill, and a self-confidence sometimes bordering on arrogance, he created a hatful of scoring opportunities.

While McCole was not one to shirk a ruck of defenders wherein elbows were flailing and boots flying if it meant the chance of a goal, he was more than a battering ram. With his speed and good control he looked the one player in the Leeds forward line always likely to score. In training, he once took it upon himself to give a less cocksure team-mate a very public lesson in the art of penalty-taking.

But while the long-term prospects at Elland Road did not look good for McCole, many were surprised by his return to Bradford City in October 1961, a month after he created a club record for Leeds, by scoring four goals in a League Cup tie against Brentford. Goal-machines of such calibre were hard to find.

BORN: Glasgow, 18.9.36. GAMES: 85. GOALS: 53.
OTHER CLUBS: Bradford City 58/9-59/60, 61/2-62/3
(88, 47); Rotherham United 62/3-64/5 (14, 5);
Newport County 64/5 (6, 2).

1959/60 - 1961/62

BOBBY CAMERON

Bobby Cameron was not, perhaps, the ideal player for Leeds United as they slid into crisis. Signed in 1959 from Queen's Park Rangers, for whom he played more than 250 games, Cameron was recruited to a struggling side that lacked direction. Manager Jack Taylor's new man brought with him a cheerful disposition but also a rather casual attitude to the game.

He was not, however lacking in ability. Cameron, a former Scottish schoolboy international, could play either at right-half or inside-forward. In his unstressed way, he liked to get involved, demanding the ball at every opportunity so he could work it forward. The Leeds United managers did not always have confidence in his more adventurous forays and sometimes sat fearful on the touchline lest his ambition come unstuck.

During 1961/2 season, Cameron's appearances dwindled and at the end of the season he joined Gravesend and Northfleet before returning briefly to league action with Southend in October 1963.

BORN : Greenock, 23.11.32.
GAMES: 64. GOALS: 11.
OTHER CLUBS: Queen's Park Rangers 50/1-58/9 (254, 56);
Southend United 63/4 (3, 0).

1959/60 - 1961/2

ALAN HUMPHREYS

Perhaps a move to Leeds in February 1960 was the worst thing an up and coming goalkeeper, looking to extend his career and build his confidence, could have done. Alan Humphreys, the successor of two old hands Roy Wood and Ted Burgin, came to Elland Road from Shrewsbury Town with the reputation of being among the best young goalkeepers outside the first division. At Leeds, however, with a shaky defence in front of him, he experienced some unnerving Saturday afternoons.

As Leeds stumbled into the second division, with defenders and the new goalkeeper often at odds, Humphreys' confidence appeared to suffer grievously. Mistakes at the back became infectious and although on a good day, he kept goal with nerve and agility, Humphreys' time at Elland Road was not happy.

When Don Revie became manager, he might have hoped for better times but Revie, intent on recruiting seasoned troopers to stop Leeds sliding into oblivion, instead brought in Tommy Younger; and when Younger had done his job, the Leeds manager turned to the promise of Gary Sprake. In August 1962, Humphreys drifted into non-league football but his career was later resurrected, in a modest way, in the lower divisions.

BORN: Chester 18.10.39.
GAMES: 44. GOALS: 0.
OTHER CLUBS: Shrewsbury Town 56/7-59/60 (32, 0);
Mansfield Town 64/5-67/8 (60, 0);
Chesterfield 68/9-69/70 (51, 0).

1959/60 - 1961/62

PETER McCONNELL

Peter McConnell, an attacking wing-half of some promise, joined Leeds as a teenager but when, after a four year wait, he broke into the first team, he found himself in a declining side lacking hunger and ambition. In a more dynamic environment he might have done better, for McConnell immediately caught the eye of the Leeds fans, showing the confidence to move forward with the ball and take long range shots at goal.

But his supporters were to see less than they may have liked of the freshness McConnell brought to midfield. He was in and out of a poor side, and had his most extended run after Don Revie took over as manager, in the 1961/2 team that became embroiled in a battled against relegation to division three.

For whatever reason, the story of Peter McConnell at Leeds was one of arrested development. Revie chose not to persist with him and the following season he left Leeds for Carlisle United, (then managed by Ivor Powell the former Leeds trainer), where his talent was allowed to develop. There, he enjoyed regular first team football for seven seasons and won a Third Division Championship medal in 1964/5.

BORN: Reddish, near Stockport, 3.3.37.
GAMES: 53. GOALS: 5.
OTHER CLUBS: Carlisle United 62/3-68/9 (273, 27);
Bradford City 69/70-70/1 (79, 0).

1958/59 - 1961/62

DON REVIE

As a player, Don Revie was past his prime when he arrived at Elland Road. He swapped one relegated club, Sunderland, for another that would nose-dive to the lower reaches of division two. Revie, the English prototype deep-lying centre-forward, whose vision and passing ability had been the vital component of Manchester City's success in the mid 1950s, was to become acquainted with hard times at Leeds. Yet he still had much to offer.

There, he played mainly at inside-right, a position for which Raich Carter who had been Revie's manager at Hull City, felt he had lacked sufficient punch. But Revie did not settle as captain because his superstitious nature convinced him he brought bad luck. Despite the inconsistency around him, Revie's skills were intact; he was a wise old hand with an ability to strike long, exact balls to the feet of colleagues, or create attacking space by short balls and flicks.

Revie was important as much for his maturity and leadership during an era of weak management at Elland Road, motivating himself and others, training harder than the slack regime demanded. During matches he cut an elegant figure, posing as if for a photograph after making one of his sweeter passes. But if Revie was not rugged, neither was he effete; and could strike a ball with terrific power when the occasion demanded.

He was, above all, a strategist, and inching towards management during his final playing years at Elland Road. That Revie was almost allowed to slip away and exercise his guiding spirit elsewhere may still cause some older Leeds fans to catch their breath.

BORN: Middlesbrough 10.7.27. GAMES: 80. GOALS: 12.
HONOURS: 6 England Caps 55-57.
OTHER CLUBS: Leicester City 46/7-49/50 (96, 25); Hull City 49/50-51/2 (76, 12);
Manchester City 51/2-55/6 (163, 37); Sunderland 56/7-58/9 (64, 15).
MANAGER: Leeds United 60/1-73/4.

1958/59 -1961/62

GERRY FRANCIS

Gerry Francis, the South African shoe-repairer who became Leeds United's first coloured footballer, may have had less speed and skill than his more famous compatriot Albert Johanneson but still provided Leeds fans with some choice moments from his operations on the right wing. Leeds tried Francis out as an amateur before signing him as a professional in July 1957. He was not in the top class of ball-playing wing men, perhaps more at ease in the second division where his sparkling show in the 3-2 victory at Lincoln in December 1960 was acclaimed by the home management as the best exhibition of wing play they had ever seen. Yet Francis had his good days in the first division too: his spectacular goal thundered in from the right flank during a 3-3 home draw against Everton in October 1959 remains etched in the memories of the 19,000 who were there.

But like many of his contemporaries, Francis struggled to find himself at a club lacking direction and heart. He was not to figure in Don Revie's long term plans and left for York City in October 1961 for what would be his final season of league football.

BORN: Johannesburg, 6.12.33.
GAMES: 50. GOALS: 9.
OTHER CLUBS: York City 61/2 (16, 4).

1959/60 - 1961/62

NOEL PEYTON

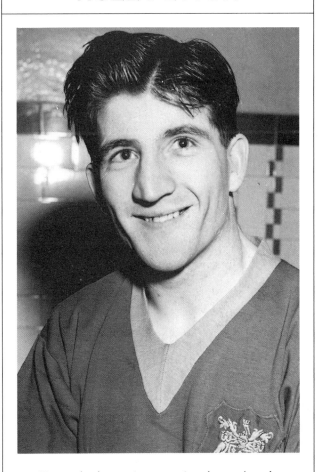

You need to be tenacious to survive when you're only five feet five with a mission to score goals. As much as anything, a love of the game and the sheer pleasure of taking to the field sustained Irish international Noel Peyton, who made most of his 105 league appearances for Leeds wearing the number 10 shirt.

His five seasons, from 1958 to 1963, were among the most trying in Leeds United's history, yet Peyton's appetite for the game was rarely dulled. A seemingly frail figure, he nevertheless showed considerable aptitude for creating good scoring positions in an era when football was less frenetic and ruthless than the modern professional game. Alas, much of the enthusiastic Peyton's approach work was squandered by his inability to score. As his team scrapped for every point during 1961/2 and the desperate dogfight to avoid division three, he scored just five times in 37 games and missed, according to one colleague, an unbelievable number of chances. Thereafter Peyton made just a handful of appearances and transferred to York City in July 1963.

BORN: Dublin 4.12.35. GAMES: 117. GOALS: 20.
HONOURS: 6 Republic of Ireland Caps 57-63.
OTHER CLUBS: Shamrock Rovers 52/3-57/8;
York City 63/4 (37, 4).

1958/59 - 1962/63

FREDDIE GOODWIN

Freddie Goodwin was among the less elegant defenders to grace Elland Road but he was a powerful stopper who might have made many more appearances for Leeds United had he not suffered a series of injuries.

Goodwin was bought from Manchester United by Jack Taylor in 1960 to plug an increasingly leaky Leeds defence. He found himself in a struggling side but few could fault his effort or commitment even to causes that sometimes seemed hopelessly lost. Although frequently wearing the number 6 shirt, Goodwin was a central defender with a bias for the right side, firm in the tackle and using his six feet one to good effect in the air.

Despite his lack of style and slowness on the turn, Goodwin - who inherited the club captaincy from Don Revie - compensated in other ways. Often hard-pressed team-mates were grateful for the vigour with which he despatched the ball away from danger areas. A stronger and harder defender than Jack Charlton in the eyes of some colleagues, Goodwin's proneness to injury prevented their defending partnership flourishing as it might have done.

Goodwin endured a devastating injury that ended his career at Elland Road: a triple fracture of the leg after colliding with his former team-mate John Charles during a third round FA Cup tie at Cardiff on January 4 1964. It was rough justice for a player who had fought many painful battles to regain fitness and his first team place.

BORN: Heywood, Lancashire, 28.6.33. GAMES: 120. GOALS: 2.
OTHER CLUBS: Manchester United 53/4-59/60 (95, 7);
Scunthorpe United 64/5 (6, 1).
MANAGER: Scunthorpe United 64/5; Brighton and Hove Albion 68/9-69/70;
Birmingham City 70/1-75/6.

1959/60 - 1963/64

TOMMY YOUNGER

The wisdom and experience brought to Leeds United by the colossal figure of nomadic goalkeeper Tommy Younger, who had reached veteran status when he arrived at Elland Road aged 31, cannot be underestimated. His career at Leeds spanned only 13 months but Younger was one of Don Revie's most important signings as he battled to revive his moribund club.

Sceptics would have put little money on the rotund Younger, who had earlier quit the game after slipping a disc while at Stoke City, being much use to Leeds United. He was reputedly slack at training and temperamental. But Younger battled to reduce his weight and applied to great effect the expertise he had gained during his peak playing days as a Scottish international with Hibernian and Liverpool in the 1950s. He was more agile than his bulk suggested, and tremendous courage and physical strength characterised Younger's performances as he helped stem the deluge of goals Leeds had been conceding.

Meanwhile, Younger's good humour and capacity for jokes, not cussedness, shone through some of Leeds' darkest days. He was a comforting figure on whom Revie occasionally felt able to lean for advice, and took the trouble to improve the skills and strength of his promising young understudy Gary Sprake. Younger's methods were typically robust; he would force the youthful keeper to catch a series of high balls while throwing a medicine ball at Sprake's body. Younger was able to retire in October 1962 knowing that while some had low expectations of him, he had helped breathe new life into Leeds United.

BORN: Edinburgh 10.4.30. GAMES: 42. GOALS: 0.
HONOURS : 24 Scotland Caps 55-58.
OTHER CLUBS: Hibernian 49/50-55/6 (177, 0);
Liverpool 56/7-58/9 (120, 0); Falkirk 59/60;
Stoke City 59/60 (10, 0).

1961/62 - 1962/63

ALBERT JOHANNESON

What might Albert Johanneson have achieved for Leeds United if he had greater self-confidence? Blessed with skills that startled some of the game's most hardened professionals, too often the coloured South African left winger's displays were diluted by self-doubt and a habit of conceding possession. Yet when he did take to the field with morale high, he could reduce opposition defences to floundering ineptitude.

Recommended to Leeds United by a South African teacher, Johanneson arrived in Yorkshire in April 1961. A diffident young man, thousands of miles away from a home culture based on racial discrimination, at first he was unsure if he was fit to jump into the bath with the other players after training. Johanneson had his answer when team-mates stripped him off and threw him in.

Despite his apprehensions, Johanneson made an immediate mark on his debut, despatching a sweet centre for Jack Charlton to head home against Swansea Town. He worked determinedly at his game and had a fine season in 1963/4 as a potent attacking force who provided 13 league goals as Leeds willed themselves to the second division championship. A Johanneson masterpiece on Easter Monday against Newcastle United, in which he brought down a long through ball and side-stepped three players before slipping the ball beyond the advancing goalkeeper, lingers in many a memory.

Perhaps his greatest disappointment came in an anaemic performance during the 1965 FA Cup Final against Liverpool. Johanneson froze on a day people anticipated his skills might torment Liverpool right-back Chris Lawler. Injuries and the emerging brilliance of Eddie Gray cut short his career at Leeds. In 1970, he left for York City, always regarded with affection by Leeds fans for illuminating much of the grimness that accompanied their club's early success.

BORN: Johannesburg, 13.3.40. GAMES: 194 (3). GOALS: 67.
HONOURS: Second Division Championship 63/4.
OTHER CLUBS: York City: 70/1 (26, 3).

1960/61 - 1969/70

TOMMY HENDERSON

Tommy Henderson, who had two spells at Leeds United, made most impact in the club's first resurgent season once the spectre of the third division had been banished. Signed as a schoolboy from Scotland in 1959, homesickness drove him back over the border but he was brought back to Elland Road by Don Revie in November 1962.

Henderson, who at five feet four could look down only on his diminutive skipper Bobby Collins, was a cheerful wholehearted player who set about training and playing with equal relish. He enjoyed a spell of 20 league matches in 1962/3 before making way for Johnny Giles the following season. His neat and sometimes tricky wing play on the right helped create a number of scoring chances as Leeds discovered the goal-touch that had eluded them for several seasons.

As Leeds reached for new heights, Henderson's opportunities became limited and he made just four league appearances the following two seasons before moving to Bury in June 1965.

BORN: Larkhall, Lanarkshire 25.7.43.
GAMES: 34. GOALS: 2.
OTHER CLUBS: Bury 65/6 (7, 1);
Swindon Town 65/6 (11, 3);
Stockport County 66/7 (19, 4).

1962/63 - 1964/65

JOHN HAWKSBY

The early burst of promise shown by winger John Hawksby was never wholly fulfilled as he struggled to make a mark during some of the most unsettled times in Leeds United's history. He was not the first (nor will he be the last) footballer to make a dramatic early impact; at 18, he scored in each of his first two games, before fading away.

Those treasured goals, coming in August 1960, were the only ones the former England youth international managed in Leeds United colours. As Jack Taylor handed over to Don Revie, Hawksby toiled on the left wing during the desperate 1961/2 season where at times he showed quite good ball control but tended to over-elaborate and concede possession.

In 1962/3, Hawksby was supplanted by Albert Johanneson in a reconstructed side that brought better days to Elland Road. In his last two seasons at Leeds, Hawksby made just nine first team appearances. He was still only 22 when his career at Leeds came to an end as, in August 1964, he moved to Lincoln and then York, helping fight rearguard actions at two clubs battling just to survive in the league.

BORN: York, 12.6.42.
GAMES: 45. GOALS: 2.
OTHER CLUBS: Lincoln City 64/5-65/6 (65, 4);
York City 65/6-67/8 (74, 7).

1960/61 - 1963/64

CLIFF MASON

While the arrival of Bobby Collins was crucial in keeping Leeds out of division three during 1961/2, the less bellicose influence of Cliff Mason, a left-back signed from Sheffield United by Don Revie to help stiffen his wobbly defence, should not be forgotten. Like Collins, Mason slotted into the team for the last eleven matches of the season, a spell when only eight goals were conceded, four in a single match at Southampton.

Mason, a former captain at Bramall Lane, was 31 when signed and he provided intelligence and experience at a troubled time for Leeds. While a less solid defender than Grenville Hair, and not as strong, he was cleverer on the ball and was sometimes overcome by the urge to dribble past opponents. His skill at the back lay in anticipation; he excelled at reading the intentions of opposing forwards and snuffing out danger.

The next season, before Grenville Hair regained his place, Mason's maturity and clear thinking were brought to bear on the raw youngsters Gary Sprake, Paul Reaney and Norman Hunter, who had been pitched prematurely into the regular grind of second division football. Though his Leeds career was short, Cliff Mason helped stopped the rot and supplied hope. The £10,000 he cost Don Revie was money well spent.

BORN: York, 27.11.29.
GAMES: 33. GOALS: 0.
OTHER CLUBS: Darlington 52/3-54/5 (107, 0);
Sheffield United 55/6-61/2 (97, 2);
Scunthorpe United 63/4 (12, 1);
Chesterfield 64/5 (5, 0).

1961/62 - 1962/63

ERIC SMITH

A double-fracture of the leg deprived Eric Smith of what might have been a more fruitful career at Elland Road. The short, stocky right-half arrived from Celtic with fire in his belly in 1960, before the start of Don Revie's management, and into what he considered was a shambles of a club.

The extrovert and outspoken Smith, who played twice for Scotland in 1959, was quick to deplore slackness. He put heart and soul into the game; every match was a personal challenge: them against him. Smith was an industrious defender, sometimes fierce in the tackle if lacking in pace, who trained hard and whose character shone through in the arduous relegation battle of 1961/2. At the same time, Smith's buoyant humour helped lighten the grimmer times. The third division may have beckoned but Eric Smith, whose premature baldness made him a distinctive figure, was rarely short of a new joke to try on his colleagues in the dressing room.

Smith's playing days at Leeds ended cruelly when he broke his leg in a tackle during a home game against Chelsea in September 1962. Two years later he was sold to Morton where he spent many years before assorted footballing jobs took him to Cyprus and the United Arab Emirates, where briefly he worked alongside his exiled former boss, Don Revie. Eric Smith died in Dubai in June 1991.

BORN: Glasgow 29.7.34. GAMES: 71. GOALS: 3.
HONOURS: 2 Scotland Caps (59).
OTHER CLUBS: Glasgow Celtic 1954/5-59/60; Morton 64/5-65/6. MANAGER: Morton 72; Hamilton Academical 72/3-77/8; Sharjah FC (United Arab Emirates) 1978.

1960/61 - 1962/63

IAN LAWSON

Don Revie was looking for goals to buttress his sagging team when he cast across the Pennines and brought Ian Lawson to Elland Road from Burnley in March 1962 for £20,000. He was not, perhaps, the most obvious choice, a no frills 23-year-old who had managed only 23 appearances during four years at Turf Moor.

Arriving as Leeds fought their desperate rearguard action to avoid relegation to the third division, Lawson was immediately drafted into the first team but scored just one league goal in eleven matches. Not until the promotion season, two years later, did he start to make an impact, contributing eleven goals in 24 matches.

Lawson, a leggy and somewhat ungainly centre-forward, played a fairly limited game, distributing the ball outfield with the aim of receiving crosses knocked into the penalty area. Though not a striker out of the top drawer, he often displayed bravery as a target man besides the intuitive goal-scorer's positional sense enabling him to score goals that might have eluded other players.

He became unsettled when, in February 1964 Alan Peacock arrived, a player of higher calibre whose signing was a statement of Revie's high ambition. Leeds United were on the threshold of a great era in which Lawson could never have played a significant part. He made just three appearances the following season and in June 1966 transferred to Crystal Palace for £9,000.

BORN: Onslow, Co Durham, 24.3.39. GAMES: 51. GOALS: 21.
HONOURS: Second Division Championship 63/4.
OTHER CLUBS: Burnley 56/7-60/61 (23, 7);
Crystal Palace 65/6 (17, 6); Port Vale 66/7 (8, 0).

1961/62 - 1964/65

DON WESTON

The itinerant Don Weston was one of those experienced, self-possessed players who gave Leeds United fans cause for optimism as the club's resurgence began. Indeed, he began his career at Elland Road in quite sensational fashion, scoring a hat trick against Stoke City during his home debut in December 1962.

Weston was one of a clutch of centre-forwards bought by Don Revie and distributed about the front-line to suit the occasion. While his opening salvo did not herald a deluge of goals, Weston was to play an important stabilising role at Elland Road. Speed and fitness were his great assets. He had, in the words of Bobby Collins, 'a turn of foot like nobody's business', and it was this pace and mobility that had attracted Don Revie. Weston could unsettle opposition defences by bringing the ball under control in midfield and launching his attacks from deep.

He was canny enough to play within his capabilities and dedicated to keeping himself in peak physical condition; a sound, unfancy player rather than an extravagant one. Though a potent figure in the 1963/4 promotion year, Weston, one of soccer's superior journeymen, faded out of the team as Leeds became a first division force and the goal-scoring talents of Alan Peacock and Jim Storrie came to the fore. He was transferred to Huddersfield Town in October 1965.

BORN: Mansfield, 6.3.36. GAMES: 78. GOALS: 26.
HONOURS: Second Division Championship 63/4.
OTHER CLUBS: Wrexham 58/9, 66/7 (84, 40);
Birmingham City 59/60 (23, 3); Rotherham United 60/2 (76, 21);
Huddersfield Town 65/6 (21, 7); Chester 68/9 (3, 0).

1962/3 - 1964/5

BOBBY COLLINS

Bobby Collins, told by Everton manager Harry Catterick he would have to fight for his first team place after years of playing like a demon, left Goodison Park in anger. When, in March 1962, the diminutive inside forward crossed the Pennines and joined Leeds United at the age of 31, the will to win had probably never burned more intensely within him. Nor, indeed, within any professional footballer.

It would have been hard for the proud Scotsman to have found a stiffer challenge. He collared a side drifting into the third division, and under his leadership, Leeds lost only one of their last eleven matches. It is no exaggeration to say that when Don Revie descended on Collins and bought him up for just £25,000, he struck the most crucially important transfer deal in Leeds United's history. It was to lead the club out of the dark ages and lay the foundation for a brilliant future.

Some might have felt Collins, who had already won 28 Scottish caps with Celtic and Everton, had seen everything, done it all. But he had an appetite and energy for the game that seemed infinitely renewable. Wearing the number eight shirt and playing as an attacking midfielder, he had tremendous vision and was a master at striking the long, penetrative ball to unlock opposition defences. While he had a powerful shot it was Collins' strength in the tackle that often stunned his opponents; his capacity to mix it with men half his size again and leave them flattened.

'Win first and take it as it comes . . . don't turn the other cheek or they'll kill you', are among Collins' mottoes. As Don Revie's general on the field, Bobby Collins' spirit is associated with some of Leeds United's more ferocious performances along their turbulent passage to the top. In his Indian Summer, he was to gain three more Scottish caps. Severe injuries, such as a broken leg, were not enough to make him quit. 'You can miss a couple of seasons . . . that happens', he says with the near-nonchalance of one who, at nearly 35, broke a leg during the Inter Cities Fairs Cup match against Torino in October 1965 yet recovered to make seven first team appearances in 1966/7 before being granted a free transfer to Bury.

Still living in Leeds and working as a freelance scout, Collins' love of the game and its players is undimmed, and the pleasure derived from a grand career that helped usher in Leeds United's first golden age still glows within him.

BORN: Glasgow 16.2.31.
GAMES: 167. GOALS: 25.
HONOURS: Second Divison Championship 63/4.
Footballer of the Year 1964/5.
31 Scotland Caps (51-65).
OTHER CLUBS: Glasgow Celtic 49/50-58/9 (220, 81);
Everton 58/9-61/2 (133, 42); Bury 66/7-68/9 (75, 5);
Morton 69/70-70/1 (54, 2); Ringwood City, Australia;
Oldham Athletic 72/3 (6, 0).
MANAGER: Huddersfield Town 74/5-75/6;
Hull City 77/8; Barnsley 84/5.

1961/62 - 1966/67

JIM STORRIE

Jim Storrie was among Don Revie's most inspired purchases. Looking for a proven goal scorer is one thing; picking one up for £15,000 who could hit the net at crucial times was quite another. Storrie began his career in the modest surroundings at Airdrie but showed at Leeds he had the calibre to adjust to any level of football asked of him.

While more than 27,000 fans turned up at Stoke to witness the return of John Charles in Leeds' opening match of 1962/3, the less-feted debutant Storrie struck the only goal of the game. But it was when Leeds returned to the first division that Storrie, free of injury, showed he could thrive on the big occasion. At less than five feet nine, he was one of the league's smaller centre-forwards, though often played at number 8, accompanying either Rod Johnson or the injury-prone Alan Peacock.

Storrie, who was popular at Elland Road as much for his genial personality as for his committed play, had a hustling hard-running style that could force defensive errors. As well as his own adroit ability to score, he had a knack of creating chances for colleagues which derived from his fearless incursions into the penalty area, where he was quick to latch on to loose balls and visualise goal-scoring opportunities.

Had not Storrie been carrying an injury in the 1965 FA Cup Final, the Leeds United attack, a shadow of itself that day, might have given the Liverpool defence a more unsettling afternoon. In the following two seasons, Jim Storrie was to fade from the first team scene as injuries, and a shortage of top drawer strikers, forced Don Revie to re-think his front line. When he left for Aberdeen in February 1967, Storrie could be satisfied he had contributed much to the ascent of Leeds United.

BORN: Kirkintilloch, Lanarkshire, 31.3.40. GAMES 153 (3). GOALS: 67.
Honours: Second Division Championship 63/4.
OTHER CLUBS: Airdrie 57/8-62/3; Aberdeen 66/7-67/8;
Rotherham United 67/8-69/70 (71, 19); Portsmouth: 69/70-71/2 (43, 12);
Aldershot *(on loan)* 71/2 (5, 1); St Mirren; 72/3 (9, 3).

1962/63 - 1966/67

WILLIE BELL

That Willie Bell would come to be regarded as an invaluable defensive pillar in the first of Don Revie's great Leeds teams had not looked likely when he arrived at Elland Road from Queen's Park in 1960. Bell was a pedestrian midfielder who found it hard to get into even a struggling side during his first two seasons. His career as a regular left-back, the position for which he is remembered, did not start until the departure of Cliff Mason and Grenville Hair. Then, with his playing career well advanced, Bell found the position to which he had seemed born.

There have been more dazzling left-backs in Leeds United's history. While he had adequate pace, Bell was not the swiftest of defenders. What he did have was endless determination and dedication. As he matured in the position, speed of thought and anticipation became Willie Bell's most valuable qualities, compensating for his occasional deficiency when he laboured to contain skilful ball-players who ran at him.

Bell also a good and determined tackler and was brave in the air. Part of his job was to challenge in the bruising, dangerous areas of the field as the spare man at the back who would attack the ball from corners and free kicks. Even as a mature player, he would listen to advice and try to find ways of improving his game. Willie Bell's efforts won him two Scottish international caps and there was still plenty of football within him when he transferred to Leicester in September 1967 to make way for the incandescent talents of Terry Cooper.

BORN: Johnstone, Lanarkshire 3.9.37. GAMES: 260. GOALS: 18.
HONOURS: Second Division Championship 63/4.
2 Scotland Caps 1966.
OTHER CLUBS: Queen's Park, 57/8-59/60;
Leicester City 67/8-68/9 (49, 0); Brighton & Hove Albion 69/70 (44, 1).
MANAGER: Birmingham City 75/6-77/8; Lincoln City 77/8-78/9.

1960/61 - 1967/68

ALF JONES

PETER FITZGERALD

BILLY McADAMS

ALF JONES 1960/61-1961/62

Right-back. BORN: Liverpool, 2.3.37. GAMES: 29. GOALS: 0.
OTHER CLUBS: Lincoln City 62/3-66/7 (178, 3).

JOHN KILFORD 1958/59-1961/62

Full-back. BORN: Derby, 18.11.38. GAMES: 23. GOALS: 0.
OTHER CLUBS: Notts County 58/9 (26, 0).

PETER FITZGERALD 1960/61

Centre-forward. BORN: Waterford, Ireland, 17.6.37.
GAMES: 8. GOALS: 0.
HONOURS: 5 Republic of Ireland Caps 1961-62.
OTHER CLUBS: Waterford, Ireland; St Patrick's Athletic,
Ireland; Sparta Rotterdam, Holland; 1960;
Chester 61/2-63/4 (80, 12).

DEREK MAYERS 1961/62

Right-wing. BORN: Liverpool, 24.1.35.
GAMES: 24. GOALS: 5.
OTHER CLUBS: Everton 52/3-56/7 (18, 7);
Preston North End 57/8-60/1 (118, 25);
Bury 62/3-63/4 (32, 6); Wrexham 63/4 (21 ,2)

BILLY McADAMS 1961/62

Centre-forward. BORN: Belfast, 20.1.31.
GAMES: 13. GOALS: 4.
HONOURS: 15 Northern Ireland Caps 54-62.
OTHER CLUBS: Manchester City 53/4-59/60 (127, 62);
Bolton Wanderers 60/1-61/2 (44, 26);
Brentford 62/3-64/5 (75, 36);
Queen's Park Rangers 64/5-65/6 (33, 13);
Barrow 66/7-67/8 (53, 9)

COLIN GRAINGER 1960/61

Left-wing. BORN: Wakefield, 10.6.33.
GAMES: 37. GOALS: 6.
HONOURS: 7 England Caps 1956-57.
OTHER CLUBS: Wrexham 50/1-52/3 (5, 0);
Sheffield United 53/4-56/7 (88, 26);
Sunderland 56/7-59/60 (120, 14);
Port Vale 61/2-63/4 (39, 6);
Doncaster Rovers 64/5-65/6 (40, 4).

JOHN KILFORD

DEREK MAYERS

COLIN GRAINGER

MIKE ADDY

TERRY CASEY

BRIAN WILLIAMSON

NIGEL DAVEY

MIKE ADDY 1961/62-1962/63

Wing-half. BORN: Knottingley, 20.2.43.
GAMES: 4. GOALS: 0.
OTHER CLUBS: Barnsley 64/5-66/7 (51, 5).

TOM HALLETT 1962/63

Half-Back. BORN: Glenneath, near Swansea, 10.4.39.
GAMES: 1. GOALS: 0.
OTHER CLUBS: Swindon Town 63/4-65/6 (26, 0);
Bradford City 66/7-70/1 (179, 2).

TERRY CASEY 1961/62

Half-back. BORN: Swansea, 5.9.43.
GAMES: 4. GOALS: 0.

TERRY CARLING 1960/61-1961/62

Goalkeeper. BORN: Otley, near Leeds, 26.2.39.
GAMES: 6. GOALS: 0.
OTHER CLUBS: Lincoln City 62/3-63/4 (84, 0);
Walsall 64/5-66/7 (101, 0);
Chester 66/7-70/1 (199, 0).

BRIAN WILLIAMSON 1963/64-1965/66

Goalkeeper. BORN: Blyth, Northumberland, 6.10.39.
GAMES: 8. GOALS: 0.
OTHER CLUBS: Gateshead 58/9-59/60 (55, 0);
Crewe Alexandra 60/1-61/2 (55, 0);
Nottingham Forest 67/8-68/9 (19, 0); Leicester City *(on loan)*
67/8 (6, 0); Fulham 68/69-69/70 (12, 0).

BARRIE WRIGHT 1962/63-1965/66

Left-back. BORN: Bradford, 6.11.45.
GAMES: 8. GOALS: 0.
OTHER CLUBS: New York Generals, USA;
Brighton and Hove Albion 68/9-69/70 (10, 0).

NIGEL DAVEY 1965/6-1971/2.

Full-back. BORN: Garforth, Leeds, 20.6.46.
GAMES: 20 (3). GOALS: 0

TOM HALLETT

TERRY CARLING

BARRIE WRIGHT

JACK CHARLTON

Some are born great, some achieve greatness. In the footballing family Charlton, it was clear Bobby had entered the world with a prodigious footballing talent. Elder brother Jack, often at odds with himself, his club, the world in general, did not excite the public as he toiled away at Elland Road. The notion that in his 30s he would be voted Footballer of the Year would have seemed fantastic in his earlier playing days.

Jack Charlton made his debut for Leeds in 1953 against Doncaster Rovers. For a time he was unsettled by the presence and versatility of John Charles who could make, seemingly at will, the centre-forward or centre-half position his own. Yet even before he escaped the shadows of greater players, it was clear Charlton had much to offer; he was swift, a first class header of the ball and a good tackler. By 1957 he was playing for the Football League against the League of Ireland.

But for the next five years, Leeds' and Charlton's fortunes slumped. As seemingly his best playing years slipped away, he was marooned in a struggling side; a capable footballer but with in-built bad habits. One soccer reporter in this period described him as starting a match as if he had just woken up from an anaesthetic.

Listening to advice and heeding the authority of his new manager Don Revie did not come easily but over some aspects of his play, Revie learned to give the wilful Charlton his head. Nothing, it seemed, could stop him embarking on loping attacking runs, in which he developed such a momentum that defences parted like the Red Sea as he charged towards goal. But Revie did drum into Charlton the need for marking opposing centre-forwards, many of whom had been coming off him and creating goal-scoring opportunities. Before, Charlton opted for sorting games out as they progressed; and not always to his team's benefit.

Suddenly, surrounded by brilliant young defenders such as Paul Reaney and Norman Hunter, Jack Charlton's career began its belated glorious surge, to the England team and the World Cup Final; to a League Championship and European triumphs. In his early thirties he became an ever-more assuring presence in defence and his aerial domination, not least his habit of standing on the opposition goal-line at corner kicks as Leeds attacked, yielded priceless goals.

Once he had seemed much the lesser of two footballing sons; a sometimes cantankerous journeyman (though not without a droll sense of humour). In the end Jack Charlton's epic 20 year career, during which he played almost 800 games in all competitions, became a triumph; and he a great football character.

BORN: Ashington, Co. Durham, 8.5.35.
GAMES: 772. GOALS: 95.
HONOURS: League Championship 68/9; FA Cup 71/2;
Inter Cities Fairs Cup 67/8; 70/1; League Cup 67/8.
Second Division Championship 63/4.
Footballer of the Year 66/7.
35 England Caps 65/70.
MANAGER: Middlesbrough 73/4-76/7;
Sheffield Wednesday 77/8-82/3;
Newcastle 84/5; Republic of Ireland 86- .

1952/53 - 1972/73

JIMMY GREENHOFF

Many Leeds United fans felt the departure from Elland Road of Jimmy Greenhoff was premature; there was a sense almost of anguish that someone with his fluid talents could not be accommodated in Don Revie's grand scheme of things.

There could scarcely have been a better advertisement for the game than Jimmy Greenhoff with the ball at his feet embarking on swift surging runs from the right side of midfield. He was, and looked, a natural footballer; yet it was at other clubs, and at centre-forward that he would eventually exploit his talents most fully.

Greenhoff's switch to a striker's role began at Leeds in 1966/7, for it was felt he lacked the stamina to spend 90 minutes covering the field from end to end. At centre-forward, his excellent control, assured first touch and intelligent distribution could be used to greater advantage - and he could get a rest when needed.

As he matured physically, Jimmy Greenhoff became an increasingly potent player, though always a cool-headed one. He was an excellent striker of the ball, capable of spectacular goals, few more so than his searing 20 yard volley which gave Leeds an early lead in the home leg of their 1967 Inter Cities Fairs Cup battle against Valencia.

The arrival of Mick Jones made Greeenhoff's position at Elland Road insecure and in August 1968 he transferred to Birmingham City for £70,000. But it was perhaps with Stoke in the early 1970s that he demonstrated his often enthralling talents to the full, in one of the Potters' most successful eras during which, in 1972, he helped them win the League Cup. Jimmy Greenhoff was one of the finest players never to win a full England cap, perhaps the price for being, in footballing terms, not quite a conformist.

BORN: Barnsley, 19.6.46. GAMES: 128 (8). GOALS: 33.
HONOURS: League Cup 67/8.
OTHER CLUBS: Birmingham City 68/9-69/70 (31, 14); Stoke City 69/70-76/7 (274, 76); Manchester United 76/7-80/1 (97, 26); Crewe Alexandra 80/1 (11, 4); Toronto Blizzards, Canada; 80/1; Port Vale 81/2-82/3 (48, 5); Rochdale 82/3-83/4 (16, 0).
MANAGER: Crewe Alexandra 80/1; Rochdale 82/3-83/4.

1963/64 - 1968/69

ALAN PEACOCK

Alan Peacock - the finest header of a ball in the country according to the then England manager Walter Winterbottom - spent too many of the precious few years a footballer has at his peak fighting injury. He had already endured his share of problems with Middlesbrough - for whom he scored 126 goals in 218 league appearances - before Don Revie brought him to Elland Road in February 1964 to add thrust to Leeds' promotion campaign.

Peacock did just that. His height, strength and fearlessness made him a menace for opposing defences. Alan Peacock made a scoring debut at Norwich during a 2-2 draw on February 8 1964 and contributed a further seven goals in Leeds' final 13 matches of the season during which only five points were dropped.

Such was his aerial ability, Peacock produced goals for others as well as scoring himself. The team leaned heavily on his strength and willingness, firing abundant crosses into the penalty area for Peacock to gobble up either as scoring chances or balls to be laid off for team-mates. He was an excellent team player, always on hand to link up with play, though sufficiently aware of his modest skills on the ball not to try things beyond him.

Much of Peacock's bravery went unseen save by colleagues and the Leeds management. He had a succession of cartilage operations, doing his utmost to regain fitness each time. Yet such was his luck, his knee gave out sooner or later. Lesser men might have had bouts of black despair but if Peacock grieved, he did so privately. He is remembered for his good cheer and humour in trying circumstances. Without him, the Leeds forward line was a blunter instrument until Mick Jones emerged to perform the task of target man so honourably.

BORN: Middlesbrough, 29.10.37.
GAMES: 65. GOALS: 31.
HONOURS: Second Division Championship 64/5.
6 England Caps 62-66.
OTHER CLUBS: Middlesbrough 55/6-63/4 (218, 126);
Plymouth Argyle 67/8 (3, 0).

1963/64 - 1966/67

GARY SPRAKE

What might Leeds United have achieved under Don Revie, were it not for Gary Sprake? How much did his aberrant performances cost them in terms of cups and championships? Such questions are posed by the Welsh goalkeeper's detractors whose numbers, including former team-mates, became ever more voluble after Sprake was involved in allegations of bribery against his former manager.

In a team where there was scarcely a weakness, whose relentless pursuit of honours kept it constantly in the public eye, Sprake could not make his blunders discreetly. Liverpool, at Anfield, scarcely needed his helping hands in 1967, in a league match they were already leading, but Sprake obliged nonetheless, throwing the ball with some impetus into his own net.

And then, say those who decry him, there was the one against Crystal Palace in 1970/1, when Arsenal pipped Leeds for the League Championship by a single point. Well in control of a 1-0 lead at Selhurst Park, three minutes remained when Sprake allowed a gentle drifting long-range shot by full-back John Sewell to sail between his arms and into the net. And Peter Houseman's goal that brought Chelsea level at 1-1 during the first match of the marathon 1970 cup final; the soft one from 25 yards that Sprake just allowed to slide beneath his body . . .

There is much material for the case against. But what of the matches that Leeds won on their way to a League Championship, two European triumphs, the League Cup, and all the near misses? What of Sprake's part in those? In truth, Gary Sprake was a goalkeeper of the highest class who made unfortunate and highly conspicuous mistakes. More often though, his handling was sure, his athleticism and bravery all that might be expected; qualities which drew from him spectacular reflex saves in crucial matches. Not much criticism of Sprake is attached to the 1968/9 season when Leeds won the first division with the fewest number of goals conceded by any champions. At the start of that season, he produced heroics to shut out Ferencvaros in Hungary, and help Leeds secure the 0-0 draw they needed to win the Inter Cities Fairs Cup for the first time.

Sprake's career was turbulent from the first when, as a 16-year-old, he was airlifted by a specially chartered flight down to Southampton to replace Tommy Younger who had been taken ill. The match, played on March 17 1962, was lost 4-1; relegation threatened. But Revie had faith in the Swansea youngster. Indeed when Sprake, homesick and lacking confidence, abandoned Elland Road and returned to South Wales, he was pursued by the Leeds manager who convinced him he had a future in the game. What prevented Sprake achieving the greatness his raw talent might have brought him was, perhaps, a troubled temperament that gave rise to lapses of concentration and flashes of temper. Eventually, he was ousted by his patient understudy David Harvey and transferred to Birmingham in 1973 where a back injury forced his premature retirement from the game. Always something of a loner, the camaraderie that remains among many of the Revie old boys is something denied to the mysterious Welshman.

BORN: Winchwen, Swansea, 3.4.45.
GAMES: 504 (2). GOALS: 0.
HONOURS: League Championship 68/9; Inter Cities Fairs Cup 67/8, 70/1;
Football League Cup 67/8; Second Division Championship 63/4.
37 Wales Caps 64-75.
OTHER CLUBS: Birmingham City 73/4 (16, 0).

1961/62 - 1972/73

BILLY BREMNER

Billy Bremner, perspiring with hair tousled and manager Don Revie's hand on his shoulder is an enduring icon from Leeds United's greatest days. Revie had visions of Leeds conquering all. Bremner was his emissary, his captain who sweated blood; almost like a son as they shared in grievous disappointment and triumphant success.

Thus, the myth. In fact, Bremner was his own man who liked a cigarette and a glass of whisky and the relationship, although one of the highest mutual respect, was not quite such a stirring tale of mutual devotion. During the dark days of his early management, Revie and Bremner rowed over whether the volatile youngster from Stirling should play in a central attacking role or, Revie's preference, wide on the right. Bremner was unsettled and homesick and wanted to move.

Keeping Bremner at Leeds was a triumph of Revie's manipulative powers. Bremner arrived at Elland Road in December 1959 and made his debut against Chelsea the following month having had, at the paternal Revie's behest, an early night beforehand. How Arsenal and Chelsea must have rued declining Bremner's services because they felt that, at five feet five, he was too small. Once Revie became Bremner's manager, with dreams of building a team around him, he threatened to walk out when directors conspired to sell him to reduce the club's debts.

Time showed Bremner had everything: terrific fitness and energy, endless stomach for a battle. Quick to the tackle, he could then produce sophisticated intelligent passes, turning defence into attack. Or, with a sudden burst of acceleration, dart deep into enemy territory and score himself. Overhead kicks, winning the ball in the air against men six inches taller, Bremner could do the lot. Small wonder Revie was desperate to keep him.

Yet Bremner might have been undone by his fiery temper. Moreover, he was easily provoked by cynical opponents and in the 1960s, his career disfigured by suspensions. Revie and the players strove to save him from himself and the malign attentions of others. But gradually Bremner matured towards greatness. The first of 54 caps for Scotland came in May 1965. Before one of his latter bouts of suspension, in October 1967, Bremner produced a bravura performance in the 7-0 mauling of managerless Chelsea at Elland Road, crowning his act with a party-piece goal from an overhead kick. In 1968, Revie thrust the team captaincy upon him. Week in, week out, Bremner produced potent if argumentative performances with the temper held in check. Just.

In 1970, when Leeds strove to win the league, FA Cup and European Cup yet ended with nothing, Bremner was voted Footballer of the Year. He still had five years at the top left in him and led Leeds to their only FA Cup triumph against Arsenal in 1972, to a second League Championship in 1974, prompting the dazzling revival of a team many thought was spent. Bremner was a Titan who, when he left for Hull City in September 1976 for £35,000, had helped create vivid, unrepeatable football history.

BORN: Stirling, 9.12.42.
GAMES: 770 (1). GOALS: 115.
HONOURS: League Championship 68/9, 73/4; FA Cup 71/2;
Inter Cities Fairs Cup 67/8; 70/1; League Cup 67/8;
Second Division Championship 63/4.
Footballer of the Year 1970. 54 Scotland Caps 65-76).
OTHER CLUBS: Hull City 76/7-78/9 (61 6);
Doncaster Rovers 78/9-80/1 (5, 0).
MANAGER: Doncaster Rovers 78/9-84/5;
Leeds United 85/6-88/9;
Doncaster Rovers 89/90-91/2.

1959/60 - 1976/77

NORMAN HUNTER

It is hard to imagine that when Norman Hunter came to Elland Road as a 15-year-old schoolboy, he was a skinny beanpole of a youth, sometimes lacking the strength to pass the ball where his best instincts told him it should be played. From such raw material blossomed one of the world's great defensive footballers, a player with unlimited heart and quite brilliant positional sense, to say nothing of his tackling. For some forwards, the sight of Norman thundering in at full throttle with the fixed intent of claiming the ball must have had all the appeal of swimming in waters inhabited by a great white shark. Once Hunter bit your legs, the memory stayed with you.

He was arguably the hardest defender in a generation that included Tommy Smith, Ron Harris and Peter Storey. If hardness means the utter commitment of his tremendous physique to win the ball, to do whatever was needed for the cause without flinching even when in pain, then perhaps he was. Hunter was occasionally ruthless, sometimes brutal, but if hardness also implies snarling, snapping and sheer nastiness, then he was usually above that sort of thing. And off the field, Norman is remembered for geniality, not malice.

Hunter's value to Leeds United's great teams of the Revie era was incalculable. His speed and anticipation frequently became his side's last line of defence if other colleagues were dragged out of position. The coherence of the Hunter-Charlton partnership in defence was one of the rocks on which Leeds' success was built. But there was more, much more, to Hunter's game than being an effective stopper. The ambition he showed as an apprentice to play a constructive passing game was fulfilled as his strength developed. Hunter's ability to play accurate raking balls that switched defence into attack is one of the less appreciated aspects of his game.

To be struck by one of Norman Hunter's fiercely driven left-foot shots was not unlike impeding the progress of a cannon ball. But although emphatically left-sided, his right boot could also despatch the occasional venomous scoring shot for club and country. As Hunter matured, other facets of his play emerged; his close control in tight positions, never better demonstrated than during the 1973 FA Cup Final in which he showed remarkable composure, delicacy even, as he dribbled past three Sunderland defenders on the edge of his penalty area before taking the ball away upfield.

Had it not been for the immovability of Bobby Moore, Hunter would have gained many more than the 28 caps he won for England. When, aged 33, he appeared to be slowing down and left Leeds United to join Bristol City, some thought he was looking for a quieter life. Yet Hunter, who had done everything in the game, approached the transfer as a fresh challenge and made a further 100 league appearances. Leeds United may never find another defender of his like, with such a combination of talent, durability, endeavour and sheer love of the game.

BORN: Eighton Banks, Co. Durham, 24.10.43.
GAMES: 722 (2). GOALS: 21.
HONOURS: League Championship 68/9; 73/4; FA Cup 71/2;
Inter Cities Fairs Cup 67/8; 70/1;
Second Division Championship 63/4.
PFA Player of the Year 1973. 28 England Caps 66-75.
OTHER CLUBS: Bristol City 76/7-78/9 (108, 4);
Barnsley 79/80-82/3 (31, 0).
MANAGER: Barnsley 80/1-83/4;
Rotherham United 85/6-87/8.

1962/63 -1976/77

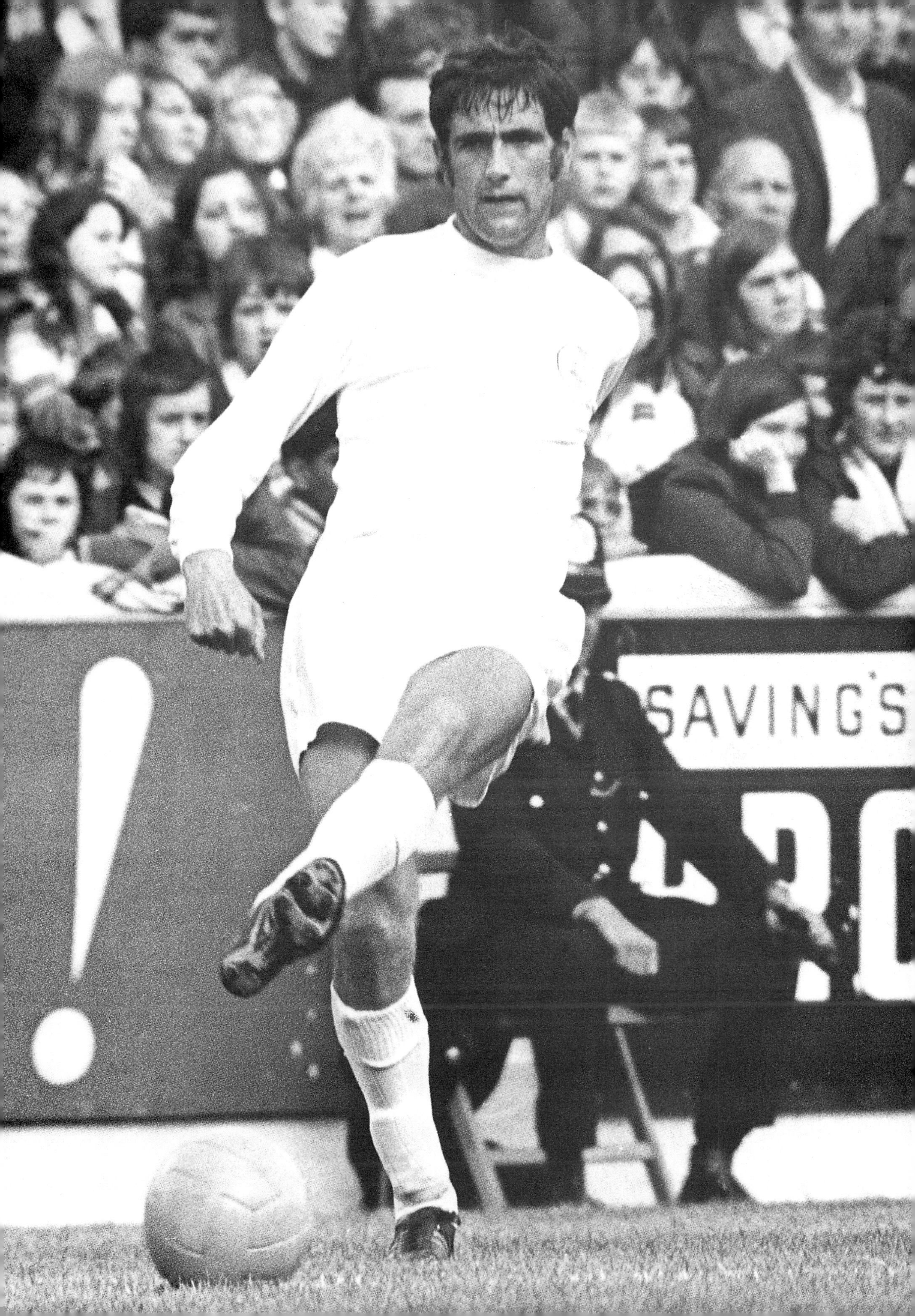
SAVING'S

TERRY COOPER

Terry Cooper's career at Elland Road burned a long fuse before it sparked into fulfilment. It took him six years at Leeds to claim a regular first team place and, considering his talents, it seems extraordinary Don Revie almost sold Cooper quite cheaply to Blackburn Rovers, unsure of how to make the best of him. The trouble was finding a niche for him. Formerly with Wolverhampton Wanderers as a junior, Cooper joined Leeds in 1961 as a left-winger but despite good ball control he was insufficiently sharp and unable to shrug off the constant close attentions of defenders. During the next four seasons, Cooper made first team appearances in fits and starts and grew increasingly frustrated with his lot.

Don Revie said it became one of his recurring nightmares that he might have let Cooper go for just £25,000. But Blackburn considered even that modest fee excessive. Eventually a solution was found: in 1967/8, Terry Cooper assumed the left-back position in place of Willie Bell, where he would have the advantage of facing play. Yet as a purely defensive left-back, Cooper had his imperfections. He was never exceptionally fast and also vulnerable when being attacked, sometimes dependent on Norman Hunter as extra cover. He was notably left-footed but that was less of a problem, for right-wingers tended to play to his stronger side.

All these flaws; yet within three years of becoming a regular, Cooper was playing in the World Cup finals in Mexico and being spoken of as the best left-back anywhere. As much as anything this was down to the exhilarating constructive role he loved to play. A shrewd player - and one with a dry sense of humour - Cooper's footballing brain was there for all to see, exemplified by his superbly timed and struck passes down the left for Eddie Gray. But Terry Cooper found his own left-winger's instinct irrepressible and was never happier than when overlapping as an extra attacker, crossing balls into the penalty area that caused panic in many defences.

Once it had developed a full momentum, Cooper's career became full of extravagant peaks - his beautifully volleyed goal which won Leeds their first major trophy, the League Cup in 1968 - and troughs, worst, the broken leg sustained during an away match against Stoke in April 1972 that robbed him not only of an FA Cup winners medal but of games in which to enthrall crowds when at the height of his powers. Cooper's emergence, as much as anything, helped Leeds shuffle off their image as a dour side. His subsequent career as manager suggests he still has much to offer football at the highest level.

BORN: Brotherton, near Castleford, West Yorkshire, 12.7.44.
GAMES: 339 (11). GOALS: 11.
HONOURS: League Championship 68/9;
Inter Cities Fairs Cup 67/8, 70/1;
League Cup 67/8.
20 England Caps 69-75.
OTHER CLUBS: Middlesbrough 74/5-77/8 (105, 1);
Bristol City 78/9 and 82/3-83/4 (70, 0);
Bristol Rovers 79/80-81/2 (59, 0);
Doncaster Rovers 81/2 (20, 0).
MANAGER: Bristol City 82/3-87/8;
Exeter City 88/9-90/1;
Birmingham City 91/2 -

1963/64 - 1974/75

PAUL MADELEY

It is hard to know with what to compare Paul Madeley, arguably the most versatile footballer of his generation. A limousine, perhaps, as he cruised in elegant fashion up and down the pitch, gobbling up the yards with great economy of effort. His ability to drop into almost any position of the field was priceless to Don Revie; yet such was the abundance of talent at Elland Road, Madeley did not have a slot of his own. Instead, he was deployed in every position except goal during his 18 seasons, though never played as an orthodox winger. Many snapshots of this most eye-catching player linger in the mind's eye; the spring-heeled athleticism with which Madeley rose to head and direct the ball, the precision of his sweeping passes; his perfect balance and general neat play. Indeed Madeley's tidiness off the pitch was legendary and, such as when he was found to hang up his pyjamas, the butt of good-humoured teasing by his colleagues.

Paul Madeley, who made his debut in 1964 following injuries to Freddie Goodwin and Jack Charlton, was probably most effective adding an extra dimension in midfield, where occasionally the maestros Bremner and Giles would lapse into a stereotyped inter-passing game the opposition was able to predict. Of all his roles, this was his favourite. The addition of Madeley's talents as ball-winner and play-maker - his surging runs in overdrive to the edge of the opposition penalty area and acutely-placed passes caused panic in many a defence - brought extra strength and variety; some critics feel the lack of them in the 1970 FA Cup Final replay against Chelsea, where instead Madeley was deployed at right-back for the injured Paul Reaney, may have cost Leeds the game.

Madeley was held in high esteem also for his modesty and consideration. One afternoon, when the Elland Road training pitch became cut up and a frost threatened, it was Paul Madeley who stayed behind to help drag a hand roller across the grass while his team-mates were in the bath. And though generally reserved, his occasional intervention in a discussion could be devastating, not least when he declared to a crisis meeting Leeds United had directors called of the players that Brian Clough was no good as the club's new manager.

While tempers frayed around him as Leeds United's seasons came to the boil, Madeley showed admirable self-control and was booked just twice in over 700 appearances. It is a rare player who denies himself the chance of playing for England in the World Cup finals yet Madeley, exhausted and drained by the disappointments of the 1969-70 season and seeing little likelihood of playing in Mexico, rejected Alf Ramsey's offer to travel as a late replacement for his injured team-mate Paul Reaney. It was typical of the self-aware, business-like approach Paul Madeley brought to matters; one that served both him and Leeds United splendidly over the years.

BORN: Leeds 20.9.44.
GAMES: 711 (13). GOALS: 34.
HONOURS: League Championship 68/9, 73/4;
FA Cup 71/2; Inter Cities Fairs Cup 67/8, 70/1.
24 England Caps 71-77.

1964/65 - 1979/80

PAUL REANEY

If George Best was the most complete footballer in Britain, then what does that make Paul Reaney, the Leeds right-back who could stifle his talents as no other defender? Many lesser players than Best, who was occasionally wont to moan about some of the unyielding Reaney's methods, ended their afternoon's toil demoralised after being subjected to his close attentions. As a last line of defence, Paul Reaney was unrivalled in his era.

The art of defending is often under-rated. Paul Reaney was among its most complete practitioners. He came to Elland Road in October 1961 as 17-year-old apprentice motor mechanic and was pitched into the Leeds first team a year later alongside Norman Hunter in the same away match against Swansea. Injuries had forced Don Revie to expose both young hopefuls to the rigours of the second division far earlier than he intended.

Both immediately established themselves. Like Hunter, among Reaney's priceless qualities were consistency and durability. He learned his trade rapidly and became first choice at right-back for the next 14 years. But, like the rest of his colleagues in defence, Reaney was not merely a destroyer. Revie and his coach Syd Owen bred their young protégés to play football and Paul Reaney did so without flamboyance but to great effect. His ability to overlap down the right and knock over teasing centres into the penalty area - Revie even deployed him as an auxiliary right-winger during the 1967 Fairs Cup Final second leg against Dinamo Zagreb - were a useful weapon in Leeds United's attacking armoury. Then, almost before anyone knew it, Reaney would have sprinted the length of the pitch to resume his task of thwarting the opposition.

If Reaney had a weakness, it was that he was not the strongest kicker of a ball. While other players could unleash long passes and venomous shots seemingly at will, Paul Reaney was generally restricted to passing with the side of his foot. But it is as a saviour in defence his great strength lay. Many times, when his team was hanging on desperately, Reaney would pop up to save the day. Such was his positional sense, he is remembered by many Leeds fans as the master of the goal-line clearance, with head, foot, or whatever.

Reaney's misfortune in breaking a leg at West Ham in April 1970, his one really serious injury, robbed him of a place in the World Cup Finals and forced him to miss much of the following season. But, like so many of his colleagues, he was made of the sternest stuff, and played on for another seven seasons after recovering.

BORN: London, 22.10.44.
GAMES: 734 (12). GOALS: 9.
HONOURS: League Championship 68/9, 73/4; FA Cup 71/2;
Inter Cities Fairs Cup 67/8; 70/1; League Cup 67/8;
Second Division Championship 63/4.
3 England Caps 69-71.
OTHER CLUBS: Bradford City 78/9-79/80 (38, 0).

1962/63 - 1977/78

ROD JOHNSON

As a junior footballer, Rod Johnson played in distinguished company. His team-mates included Paul Madeley and Paul Reaney - and also Kevin Hector who became a great goal-scoring force at Derby County. Johnson, along with Madeley and Reaney, was propelled into league football in the fateful game at Swansea Town in September 1962 which, though perhaps no-one appreciated it at the time, would help lay the foundations of Revie's early great side.

Johnson must have had high hopes the match would launch his career as it did those of his debutant team-mates. Playing at centre-forward, he scored but then had the misfortune to be carried off with an injury. Thereafter, during six seasons at Elland Road, he never had an extended run in the first team.

Some senior professionals at Elland Road thought Johnson might have achieved more than he did. When in 1964/5 Leeds arrived in the first division, Johnson, with Alan Peacock injured, was given a few games at centre-forward. One was away to Manchester United, a match in which he ran rings round the experienced Bill Foulkes. But generally, Johnson was insufficiently robust to wear down first division centre-halves.

Yet he was quick and nimble, adept at bringing other players into the game as well as taking up good scoring positions himself. But first team opportunities dried up and in March 1968, he transferred to Doncaster Rovers before subsequently joining Rotherham United and Bradford City.

BORN: Leeds, 8.1.45. GAMES: 25 (5). GOALS: 6.
OTHER CLUBS: Doncaster Rovers 67/8-70/1 (107, 23);
Rotherham United 70/1-73/4 (110, 8);
Bradford City 73/4-78/9 (192, 16).

1962/63 - 1967/68

ROD BELFITT

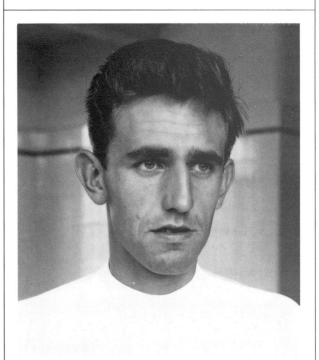

The name of Rod Belfitt is frequently mentioned in the same breath as that of his friend Mick Bates. Both spent years on the periphery of the Leeds first team yet, when drafted in to do their duty, gave creditable performances. Belfitt was a vigorous front-runner doing a sound if unspectacular job at centre-forward until the arrival of Mick Jones in September 1967.

The two strikers invited comparison from which Belfitt, in some ways, suffered. While a good header of the ball, he was not as awesome in the air as Jones. In many respects, Belfitt played a similar game, shielding the ball and relying for service on those around him. While somewhat over-dependent on his right foot, Belfitt nevertheless had a good touch and was adept at playing neat short balls.

If speed over a long distance was not his greatest asset, Belfitt had the quality striker's hallmark of responding rapidly to scoring opportunities in the penalty area. Like Bates, he enjoyed one of his most glorious moments in European competitions, when scoring a hat trick in the Inter Cities Fairs Cup semi-final first leg against Kilmarnock. But by November 1971, after eight years at Leeds, he was impatient - unlike Bates - for regular first team football and transferred to Ipswich for £55,000, the first stage of a nomadic career that followed his seven seasons at Elland Road.

BORN: Doncaster 30.10.45. GAMES: 104 (23). GOALS: 33.
HONOURS: Inter Cities Fairs Cup 67/8; League Cup 67/8.
OTHER CLUBS: Ipswich Town 71/2-72/3 (40, 13);
Everton 72/3-73/4 (16, 2); Sunderland 73/4-74/5 (39, 4);
Fulham (on loan) 74/5 (6, 1);
Huddersfield Town 74/5-75/6 (34, 8).

1964/65 - 1971/72

MIKE O'GRADY

While injuries stifled the flow of Mike O'Grady's career at Elland Road, he must have derived rich consolation from one glorious season, 1968-9, in which his bravura displays on the right wing helped bring the League Championship to Leeds for the first time.

Leeds is O'Grady's home city and he excelled there in schools soccer yet it was Huddersfield Town who, in 1959, moved smartly to bring him into professional football. So rapid was his progress, he won his first England cap and scored twice against Northern Ireland in October 1962 just nine days after his 20th birthday. Leeds recovered him from their local rivals three years later, paying £30,000.

In full flight, Mike O'Grady cut an impressive figure as a winger. He was unusually tall - a shade under five feet ten - and athletic with excellent balance. The confidence that comes from being a regular first team player brought out his manifold talents. O'Grady had a great appetite for taking on defenders, and would obey instincts to do so even if sometimes it meant losing the ball. It was not his way to search round for a team-mate to pass to, having run out of nerve or inspiration.

Mike O'Grady could be as potent a winger as any when fuelled with such self-belief. He would play with the attitude that no-one was good enough to take the ball off him and was sometimes frustrated by Don Revie's strictures on the need for caution when, in O'Grady's view, the opposition was there to be taken apart.

His excellent performances for Leeds in 1968/9 brought a second England cap, against France, yet for reasons he never fully understood, O'Grady found himself out of favour with Revie as the next season started. He transferred to Wolves where he continued to be dogged by injury. A career that promised so much flowered only briefly, and left a sense of sorrow that it was so swift to fade.

BORN: Leeds 11.10.42. GAMES: 120 (1) GOALS: 16.
HONOURS: League Championship 68/9. 2 England Caps 62-69.
OTHER CLUBS: Huddersfield Town 59/60-65/6 (160, 26);
Wolverhampton Wanderers 69/70-71/2 (32, 6);
Birmingham City (on loan) 71/2 (3, 0);
Rotherham United 72/3-73/4 (24, 2).

1965/66 - 1969/70

TERRY HIBBITT

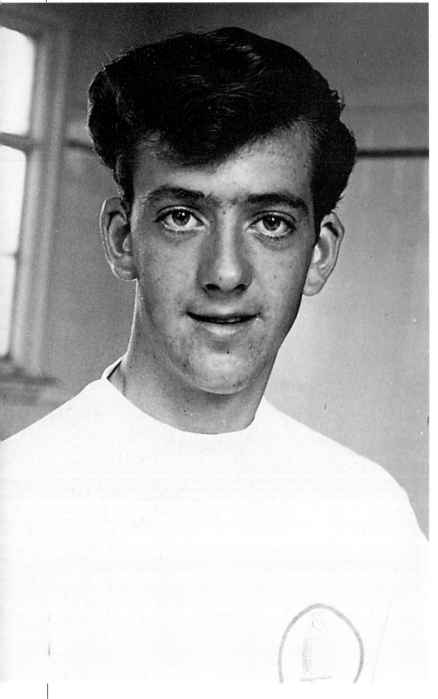

It says much for the wiles of Don Revie's management that he kept a man of Terry Hibbitt's ability content to be in the shadows at Elland Road for so long. For Hibbitt was another occasional player who, when he decided he was worth a regular first team place elsewhere, proved a fine footballer. He is not remembered at Elland Road solely for his skills: Hibbitt had the reputation of being the only Leeds player who dared cheek the godfatherly Revie.

Terry Hibbitt might have hoped for a greater future at Elland Road, following a spectacular debut when he scored in a 4-0 victory at Nottingham Forest after coming on as substitute. His ability as a left-sided midfielder was manifest but it was his misfortune to be eclipsed by Eddie Gray. Generally, only injuries to Gray allowed Hibbitt anything approaching a run in the first team.

Certainly such an elegant player - his performances were described by one critic as deliciously wispy - deserved more regular outings. Hibbitt could produce sweeping intelligent passes with his left foot as sweet as those of Giles and Hunter. But in his Leeds days, he was considered unable to cope with the physical demand of the team's unrelenting seasons as they campaigned for honours on all fronts.

For several years, Hibbitt, who amid all the intensity at Elland Road showed a cheery approach to the game, was confined mostly to the reserves. He started fewer than 50 matches but when a £30,000 move took him to Newcastle in 1971, belatedly his talents were brought centre-stage where he caught the eye as a fine supplier of ammunition for the marauding Malcolm MacDonald. It was no less than he deserved.

BORN: Bradford, 1.12.47. GAMES: 46 (17). GOALS: 11.
HONOURS: Inter Cities Fairs Cup 67/8.
OTHER CLUBS: Newcastle United 71/2-75/6 (138, 7);
Birmingham City 75/6-77/8 (110, 11);
Newcastle United 78/9-80/1 (90, 5).

1966/67 - 1970/71

JIMMY LUMSDEN

DENNIS HAWKINS

PAUL PETERSON

JOHN SHAW

BOBBY SIBBALD

CHRIS GALVIN

M. KEITH EDWARDS

M.KEITH EDWARDS 1971/72

Full-back. BORN: Neath, 26.9.52. GAMES: 0 (1). GOALS: 0.

JIMMY LUMSDEN 1966/67-1969/70

Inside-forward. BORN: Glasgow, 7.11.47.
GAMES: 3 (1). GOALS: 0.
OTHER CLUBS: Southend United 70/1 (13, 0); Morton 71/2-
72/3 (42, 3); St Mirren 72/3 (13, 1); Cork Hibernians, Ireland; 73;
Clydebank 75/6, (24, 1). ASSISTANT MANAGER: Leeds United
82/3-85/6; MANAGER: Bristol City 90/1-91/2.

BOBBY SIBBALD 1966/67-1967/68

Full-back. BORN: Hebburn, Co. Durham, 25.1.48.
GAMES: 1 (1). GOALS: 0.
OTHER CLUBS: York City 68/9 (79, 7);
Southport 71/2-76/7 (240, 13); Los Angeles Aztecs, USA.

DENNIS HAWKINS 1965/66 - 1967/68

Forward. BORN: Swansea, 22.10.47. GAMES: 4. GOALS: 0.
OTHER CLUBS: Shrewsbury Town 68/9-69/70 (62, 9); Chester
70/1 (8, 1); Workington 71/2 (6, 1); Newport County 72/3 (9, 1).

DAVID KENNEDY 1969/70-1970/71

Centre-half. BORN: Sunderland, 30.11.50. GAMES: 3. GOALS: 1.
OTHER CLUBS: Lincoln City 71/2 (8, 1).

PAUL PETERSON 1969/70

Left-back. BORN: Luton, 22.12.49. GAMES: 3 (1). GOALS: 0
OTHER CLUBS: Swindon Town 71/2 (1, 0).

CHRIS GALVIN 1969/70-1972/73

Winger. BORN: Huddersfield, 24.11.51.
GAMES: 11 (5). GOALS: 2. OTHER CLUBS: Hull City 73/4-
78/9 (143, 11); York City (on loan) 76/7 (22, 6); Stockport County
78/9-80/1 (68, 3). MANAGER: Taun Wan FC, Hong Kong, 1981.

JOHN SHAW 1971/72-1973/74

Goalkeeper. BORN: Stirling, 4.2.54.
GAMES: 2. GOALS: 0.
OTHER CLUBS: Bristol City 76/7-83/4 (295, 0);
Exeter City 85/6-87/8 (109, 0).

JOHNNY GILES

It seemed a strange move. Johnny Giles, fresh from winning a Cup Final medal with Manchester United in 1963 turned his back on Old Trafford and its ill-assorted collection of stars for a club that had not much of a past and no guaranteed future. When Don Revie persuaded Giles to move to Leeds, the rot had been stopped at Elland Road, yet there was no sign that playing there might ever become the stuff of which dreams are made.

Yet like Bobby Collins, whose position he was to fill with dazzling distinction, Giles felt he had a point to prove; that he had been unappreciated. He walked into a team he found tactically naive so his guile and experience at the top was invaluable as, in 1963/4, Leeds United grew up rapidly and forced their way to the Second Division championship.

Dublin-born Giles arrived as a right-winger and spent more than two seasons as such before switching to inside-left after Bobby Collins broke his leg against Torino in October 1965. Playing alongside Billy Bremner in midfield, it was hard to imagine a more formidable opponent. Few, if any contemporaries, displayed a comparable ingenuity at creating time and space before delivering long balls of piercing accuracy that could instantly reduce an opposing defence to a shambles. Yet this was a skill that had to be worked on, for to begin with, Giles tended to play too many short balls backwards and square

In many ways, Giles epitomised Leeds United's cold-eyed merciless approach to their victims. He could dispense physical punishment along with the best. A collision with Johnny Giles was not to be taken lightly and he was wilier at escaping the referee's attention than the more volatile Bremner. Giles' temperament made him the ideal penalty-taker and he converted spot-kicks into goals with languid, almost contemptuous coolness. When opposing teams were already on their knees, Johnny Giles would most likely supervise their extermination. His insolent flicked back-heel as his team, 7-0 up against Southampton, played a mocking keep-ball game, is relished by all Leeds fans with a twist of sadism in their make-up.

Through each of Leeds' arduous seasons, Giles matured until he became a player of world class. His tactical awareness, occasional ruthlessness, and will to win were recognised by Don Revie as essential managerial qualities. Speculation as to what success Giles might have brought Leeds had the club's directors followed Revie's advice and appointed him successor in 1974 is an enduring topic of great debate among the Elland Road faithful. Instead, West Bromwich and the Republic of Ireland became the beneficiaries of Giles' great talents.

BORN: Dublin, 6.1.40. GAMES: 521 (4). GOALS: 115.
HONOURS: League Championship 68/9, 73/4; FA Cup 71/2;
Inter Cities Fairs Cup 67/8, 70/1; League Cup 67/8;
Second Division Championship 63/4.
60 Republic of Ireland Caps 60-79.
OTHER CLUBS: Manchester United 59/60-62/3 (98, 10);
West Bromwich Albion 75/6-76/7 (75, 3); Shamrock Rovers.
MANAGER: Republic of Ireland 73-80; West Bromwich Albion 75/6-76/7;
Shamrock Rovers 77/8; West Bromwich Albion 83/4-85/6.

1963/64 - 1974/75

MICK JONES

In the seasons after Leeds United's triumphant return to the first division, it became clear the team was increasingly blunt as an attacking force. A long-term injury to Alan Peacock forced Don Revie to make experiments at centre-forward, none wholly successful. Supporters grew restive; some felt Revie was dithering. Not until September 1967 did he respond to the clamour for a big money signing, spending £100,000, then a club record, on Mick Jones.

The less than glamorous Jones may not quite have been what Leeds' more demanding fans had in mind. The Sheffield United centre-forward was a raw, unfinished product who appeared to lack basic ball control. Revie arranged special training sesssions in which the willing Jones was forced to hold the ball when closely marked. He learned this part of his craft rapidly and, using his strength to advantage, became a master of shielding the ball under pressure until his colleagues could be brought into play.

But if Jones lacked some of the game's nicer skills, he was almost foolhardily brave and willing to chase any cause. With apparent disregard for his safety, Mick Jones would interpose his head or a boot anywhere he thought necessary for the good of his team. With the arrival of Allan Clarke two seasons later there was forged the first division's most deadly striking partnership. Jones' role, by holding the ball up, chasing down the flanks or contesting balls in the penalty area was to cause defences maximum disruption, creating chances for the predatory Clarke to gobble up.

It was a job he did to perfection. There are few better examples of the two in concert than when Leeds played at Swindon in the FA Cup quarter final of 1970, Jones charging half the length of the field and shrugging off four defenders before chipping over an exquisite cross from near the left corner-flag for Clarke to head his second goal. In the ill-fated Final replay against Chelsea, the emphasis was different but equally effective : Clarke weaving a stylish pattern past three men in midfield before releasing Jones who bore down on goal past Dempsey and McCreadie to fire a goal that proclaimed his recently-acquired composure.

Jones could, of course, make and score his own goals. He had great ability in the air, in timing jumps and in the power he applied to his headers. These qualities and his nerve were seen when he launched himself between two defenders at the near post for a memorable goal at home to West Ham in November 1973 as Leeds built up a head of steam for their run of 29 league games without defeat from the start of the season.

Playing this way, he was always vulnerable to injury. The sight of the modest, softly-spoken Mick Jones struggling up the steps to the royal box for his FA Cup winners medal in 1972 somehow encapsulated a selfless career which was ended prematurely by a knee injury three years later. He had served Leeds nobly.

BORN: Worksop, Nottinghamshire, 24.4.45.
GAMES: 307 (5). GOALS: 111.
HONOURS: League Championship 68/9, 73/4; FA Cup 71/2;
Inter Cities Fairs Cup 67/8, 70/1.
3 England Caps 65-70.
OTHER CLUBS: Sheffield United 62/3-67/8 (149, 63).

1967/68 - 1973/74

JOHN FAULKNER

John Faulkner is remembered less for his appearances with Leeds United - he played just four times - than for the romantic circumstances in which he joined the club. He was playing for non-league Sutton United when their heroic progress in the 1970 FA Cup delivered a fourth round home tie against Leeds. The finest team in the land posed myriad threats to the part-timers' defence, not least through centre-forward Mick Jones whose hard running and aerial power caused many a rearguard to become misshapen and leak goals.

Faulkner's assignment was to subdue Jones. This he managed with such distinction that Don Revie, whose thoughts were turning towards cover for the ageing Jack Charlton, took notice. Intoxicated by his triumph, Faulkner went on television to tell the world he had played against better centre-forwards than Jones in his time.

Revie signed him up. Alas, Faulkner marked his first game in April 1970, at home to Burnley, with an own goal. In his second, a fortnight later, against Manchester City, he fractured a kneecap after colliding with Glyn Pardoe. The following season proved Jack Charlton, at 35, was still full of life, and Faulkner played just twice more for Leeds, against Lierse SK in the Inter Cities Fairs Cup, before moving to Luton Town in March 1972. There he enjoyed better fortune and made over 200 league appearances for the Hatters.

BORN: Orpington, Kent, 10.3.48. GAMES: 4. GOALS: 0.
OTHER CLUBS: Luton Town 71/2-77/8 (209, 6).

1969/70 - 1971/72

ROY ELLAM

Roy Ellam, bought by Don Revie as part of a small job-lot from Huddersfield Town along with Trevor Cherry, arrived at Elland Road in 1972 with hopes of replacing Jack Charlton at centre-half. But there was still a season's life in the old warhorse and, breathing down Ellam's neck, was the raw young colossus Gordon McQueen, signed a few months afterwards.

Having played more than 350 games as a first team regular at Bradford City then Huddersfield - where he had won a Second Division Championship medal two seasons earlier - life in the reserves was a new and not wholly palatable experience for the seasoned Ellam. His first match was something of a team disaster - a 4-0 defeat at Chelsea in which David Harvey was injured and Peter Lorimer put in goal.

Although six feet tall, it was clear from some of his occasional appearances that Ellam was a player of moderate ability who lacked Charlton's or even Paul Madeley's authority in the air to win high balls and despatch them smartly from the danger area. When Gordon McQueen's talents matured sufficiently, it was clear Ellam had no future at Elland Road and he returned to Huddersfield in July 1974.

BORN: Hemsworth, Yorkshire, 13.1.43.
GAMES: 19 (2). GOALS: 0.
OTHER CLUBS: Bradford City 61/2-65/6 (149, 12);
Huddersfield Town 65/6-71/2 and 74/5 (225, 10).

1972/73 - 1973/74

MICK BATES

Maybe Mick Bates was too modest for his own good. A neat and stylish left-sided midfielder, unquestionably of first division calibre, he spent twelve years at Elland Road in the shadows of Billy Bremner and Johnny Giles, playing as a stop-gap, though often with distinction when called upon because of either injury to his mentors or Don Revie's calculated game plan.

However well he might perform, the equable Bates, who played over 150 times in all competitions, generally accepted he would be restored to the reserves when Leeds United's master schemers were fit. It was not his way to go banging on the manager's door in a fit of pique when up the team sheet went and he saw his name was excluded.

How Bates might have developed elsewhere is open to question. While an excellent passer of the ball, he lacked, despite his best efforts, the quality and vision of Bremner and Giles, though the latter helped iron out faults in Bates' game, among them a tendency to chase the ball around the field and become exhausted long before full-time. Mick Bates also scored remarkably few goals for a midfielder - just four in 121 league appearances.

Bates' contentment at merely being part of English football's finest squad and the lack of a mean and hungry streak confined him to the fringes of great things. Yet he had flashes of glory, no more so than when he took the field as substitute during the 1971 Inter Cities Fairs Cup Final and, with his first kick, scored an away goal in a 2-2 draw with Juventus that proved crucial in bringing the trophy to Elland Road.

As Revie's great side disintegrated in the mid 1970s, Mick Bates went with it, transferring to Walsall in June 1976 where, still only 29, he became captain. Thereafter, his career petered out in the lower divisions, first at Bradford City then finally with Doncaster Rovers.

BORN: Doncaster 19.9.47.
GAMES: 151 (36). GOALS: 9.
HONOURS: Inter Cities Fairs Cup 67/8, 70/1.
OTHER CLUBS: Walsall 76/7-77/8 (85, 4);
Bradford City 78/9-79/80 (56, 10);
Doncaster Rovers 80/1 (4, 0).

1966/67 - 1975/76

PETER LORIMER

There were times when goalkeepers were untroubled by Peter Lorimer's fiendish shooting power. He would strike the ball with such ferocity there was no time even to glimpse it flashing through the air. No despairing dive was required; all the energy needed was to bend down and retrieve it from the net.

It may be of interest - though perhaps little consolation - to goalkeepers of Peter Lorimer's era that his high velocity shots issued from a dainty right foot. A player born to strike the ball with power and precision, Lorimer's end-of-season 176 goal tally for his school in Dundee more resembled a cricket score and cost his father a shilling a time. And while his other skills were less artistic than those of Eddie Gray, as Lorimer matured, he became a right-winger fit to grace any occasion.

By the end of his career at Elland Road, the two spells of which spanned 24 years, Peter Lorimer supplanted John Charles as the club's top scorer. At 15 years 289 days, he was Leeds United's youngest debutant. But apart from his booming shot, he had much else to offer. Whereas Eddie Gray on the left created havoc by turning defenders inside out before cutting back the ball from the by-line, Lorimer's telling contribution from the right flank was his pin-point accurate centres from which Mick Jones and Allan Clarke made hay. And if he could not match Gray for weaving intricate patterns in confined spaces, Lorimer still had the speed of wit, balance and ball control to take him past many a defender. When Leeds were in their irresistible swinging rhythm, his passing was as fine as anyone's.

At times, Peter Lorimer, who was untroubled by big match nerves, could be profligate and out of sorts, spurning some close-range chances as Leeds mauled their opposition. He revelled in and excelled in producing what he knew the crowds loved to see, making the ball sing through the air when he struck it either with his full effortless force, or chipped it with a showman's panache.

Lorimer hated losing, loathed being out of the team and grew morose in the short close season when there was no training, no football to assuage his appetite. In his second spell at the club, from 1983 to 1985, he became a more stately midfielder whose experience greatly benefited the stylish young team Eddie Gray was assembling. He was almost 39 when he played his last game. Leeds United have had fewer more durable and talented servants.

BORN: Dundee, 14.12.46.
GAMES: 674 (27). GOALS: 237.
HONOURS: League Championship 68/9, 73/4; FA Cup: 71/2;
Inter Cities Fairs Cup 67/8, 70/1; League Cup 67/8.
21 Scotland Caps 70-76.
OTHER CLUBS: Toronto Blizzards, Canada, 1979;
York City 79/80 (29, 8);
Vancouver Whitecaps, Canada, 1980.

1962/63 - 1978/79 & 1983/84 - 1985/86

TREVOR CHERRY

Trevor Cherry, while lacking the intricate, dazzling skills of Terry Cooper whom he replaced at left-back for Leeds United, nevertheless had a distinguished career out of football, making maximum use of his best qualities. Coming to Elland Road from Huddersfield Town forced him to raise the standard of his game, surrounded as he was by players of such high calibre. By his second season, he looked a worthy component of a Championship-winning side.

Cherry was signed in the summer of 1972 for £100,000 as a central defender but during 10 years at Leeds played various defensive and midfield positions. Essentially, he was a hard-tackling ball-winner with attacking instincts rather than an inspirationally creative player; and armed with a powerful shot that habitually caught opposition defences off-guard.

With his speed, application, willingness to run as long as the cause demanded, and steady temperament, Cherry settled in quickly at Leeds. Sometimes, his tackling was a touch reckless in true Norman Hunter 'they shall not pass' style; he collected nine bookings in his first season at Leeds compared with six in the previous eight at Huddersfield. Yet the assurance with which Cherry slotted in around his colleagues and stiffened the Leeds rearguard says much for his often underrated defensive skill.

In time, and as Revie's great Leeds United side disintegrated around him, Trevor Cherry, as team captain, became a focal point ; and where once he had great players all around off whom to bounce, he became one of the rocks of a lesser team. Twenty-seven England caps - perhaps more than some might have expected - came as Cherry's career progressed through the 1970s. While only an occasional goal-scorer, one strike remains among Elland Road's treasured memories : his effort in February 1977 that knocked Manchester City out of the fifth round of the FA cup three minutes from time. It was not a thing of beauty: a slightly mishit shot after an awkward, stumbling run; but no goal since has been received with such rapture by so big a Leeds crowd.

BORN: Huddersfield 23.2.48.
GAMES: 476 (8). GOALS: 31.
HONOURS: League Championship 73/4.
27 England Caps 76-80.
OTHER CLUBS: Huddersfield Town 65/6-71/2 (186, 10);
Bradford City 82/3-84/5 (92, 0).
MANAGER: Bradford City 82/3-86/7.

1972/73 - 1982/83

DAVID HARVEY

David Harvey suffered to became a goalkeeper of international standard. It looked at one time as if he might spend his entire Elland Road career as understudy to Gary Sprake whose natural talents were so eye-catching. Where Sprake had an innate ability to command the goal area and great anticipation, Harvey laboured. He did, however, have strength, dedication, courage and a phlegmatic temperament. On these qualities the once lackadaisical junior drew during his slow haul to the top. Harvey subjected himself to considerable physical punishment so he might toughen up more quickly: he threw himself about on gym mats placed in a club car park appearing in the team bath afterwards covered with bruises. He felt such self-infficted torture was necessary if he were to make the grade.

Leeds-born David Harvey signed professional for the club in February 1965 as a 17-year-old. He made his debut seven months later, in a League Cup tie against West Bromwich Albion, but thereafter made just over 30 first team appearances in seven seasons and 200 in the reserves. That Harvey tolerated this - when he did request a transfer, Don Revie's asking price deterred would-be buyers - says much about his disposition and, yet again, Revie's man-management. But as Harvey waited in the wings, some of Gary Sprake's performances became a source of anxiety in which increasingly, he undid his good work with a single ghastly lapse.

It was perhaps a strategic failure by Revie not to introduce Harvey into the first team sooner, not least because he seemed able to concentrate for 90 minutes. While his first appearance in Leeds reserves ended with a 6-0 defeat, an early first-team appearance saw him concede seven against West Ham in the League Cup and his first match as Sprake's heir in August 1972 saw him carried off at Chelsea, Harvey was to occupy the goal with understated distinction. Brave, strong, now mature and sometimes showing great athleticism, his contribution was as important as anyone's in the following Championship season.

David Harvey endured to make 350 league appearances for Leeds. The latter of these came in early 1980s, when after a spell in Canada, he was restored to Elland Road by Eddie Gray and made captain. An unlikely and perhaps ill-placed skipper, Harvey nevertheless brought experience and authority to a young defence that had yet to gel. With Peter Lorimer also back in midfield, the sight of the two old professionals playing in half-empty stadia conveyed ghostly flickers of a greater past.

BORN: Leeds 7.2.48.
GAMES: 444 (2). GOALS: 0.
HONOURS: League Championship 73/4; FA Cup 71/2.
16 Scotland Caps 73-77.
OTHER CLUBS : Vancouver Whitecaps, Canada;
Drogheda; Bradford City 84/5 (6, 0).

1965/66 - 1979/80 & 1982/83 - 1984/85

ALLAN CLARKE

Of all the great post-war English strikers, none have attracted the epithets that became attached to Allan Clarke, the second and most famous of five Staffordshire-born footballing brothers. He was spoken of not so much as a finisher than as an executioner or an assassin, as performing his job with chilling efficiency. Whatever tumult there was around him, the lean and angular Clarke would bear down on goal, seemingly without a nerve in his body, to tease out goalkeepers then slide the ball past them, lob the ball over them; or waltz round them before steering the ball into an empty net.

Few players were quicker off the mark to exploit their predatory instincts than Allan Clarke. No defence at home or abroad was safe from his speed of acceleration, his first touch, his hunter's responses to a whiff of weakness. He was served splendidly by his colleagues, none more so than Mick Jones, whose selfless hustling style drew so much of the enemy's fire.

But Clarke could do his own hustling and snapping at defenders' heels to gain possession. There was seemingly no way in which he could not score, whether he stroked the ball with his right foot, or, as against Leicester City in 1975/6, turned swiftly to volley with his left; or, if necessary, swivelled a full circle to wrong-foot a clutch of defenders before stabbing the ball home.

Allan Clarke had an unmatched ability to place the ball where it would hurt; hard, low, and away from the goalkeeper. And, of course, a similar ability when it came to heading home the ball at knee height: of all the efforts in his stylish portfolio, Allan Clarke's winning strike against Arsenal in the Centenary FA Cup Final of 1972 is the single goal most cherished by Leeds fans.

While the striker's role was his natural habitat, Clarke had shown his capabilities elsewhere on the pitch with a stirring midfield performance for Leicester City in the FA Cup Final against Manchester City in 1969, a few months before coming to Elland Road. He learned much of his passing craft at a previous club, Fulham, where his mentors were Johnny Haynes and George Cohen. Clarke's transfer fee of £165,000 was, at the time, a Football League record, but Don Revie had bought a complete footballer and goal-scorer with his finest years to come. Expensive, yes, but Allan Clarke was also one of Revie's great bargains.

BORN: Willenhall, Staffordshire, 31.7.46.
GAMES 359 (5). GOALS: 151.
HONOURS: Football League Championship 68/9, 73/4; FA Cup 71/2;
Inter Cities Fairs Cup 70/1.
19 England Caps 1970-6.
OTHER CLUBS: Walsall 63/4-65/6 (72, 41);
Fulham 65/6-67/8 (85, 45);
Leicester City 68/9 (36, 12);
Barnsley 78/9-79/80 (47, 15).
MANAGER: Barnsley 78/9-80/1;
Leeds United 80/1-81/2;
Scunthorpe United 83/4; Barnsley 85/6-89/90;
Lincoln City 90/1.

1969/70 - 1977/77

TERRY YORATH

Compared with his illustrious team-mates, Terry Yorath - a converted rugby union scrum half from South Wales - seemed an artless and ordinary footballer. Leeds United fans were used to the best and showed scant appreciation for anything less. Yet Yorath is underrated as a courageous and committed left-sided midfield player who contributed to Leeds United's success, not least in the League Championship season of 73/4, when, during his 28 matches, he filled five positions.

Of course, playing at number 10, he was not remotely in the Johnny Giles class when it came to passing and vision. But there was more to his game than the acrimonious hustling and tackling for which he is remembered. Yorath though, who was drawn to Leeds' attention by Jack Pickard, the scout who sent John Charles and Gary Sprake to Elland Road, was to serve a long apprenticeship; and learned much about the arts of fine and coarse tackling during his early years when sharing digs with Norman Hunter.

Yorath signed professional in April 1967, waiting more than five years for more than a smattering of first team chances. When in 72/3, injuries and suspensions gave him regular opportunities, he was pitched into the pressure and tumult that comprised a typical treble-chasing Leeds United season. His early games showed a mixture of vigorous composure and erratic mediocrity; it was also clear that pace was not his greatest asset.

Yet Yorath persisted and flourished. The following season he was making and scoring fine goals; in 1973/4, an adroit lob in the 3-0 victory at Ipswich; the following season a wonderful flick, controlled return and shot from the edge of the penalty area against Stoke showed his skills emerging. In crossing, passing and working openings, he also showed improvement. While Yorath's career for Wales - always somewhat impoverished of good players - took off precociously, in time, guts and effort allowed him to stand alongside the best. Later he gave sterling service to Coventry and Tottenham Hotspur.

BORN: Cardiff 27.3.50. GAMES: 165 (32). GOALS: 12.
HONOURS: League Championship 73/4. 59 Wales Caps 70-81.
OTHER CLUBS: Coventry City 76/7-78/9 (99, 3); Tottenham Hotspur 79/80-80/1 (45, 1);
Vancouver Whitecaps, Canada; Bradford City 82/3-84/5 (27, 0).
MANAGER: Wales, 1988- ; Swansea City 86/7-88/9 and 90/1; Bradford City 88/9-89/90.

1967/68 - 1976/77

DAVID STEWART

If David Harvey had good reason to curse Gary Sprake's primacy in the Leeds goal, so in turn did David Stewart come to lament Harvey's consistency as he languished for years in United's reserve team.

In five years at Elland Road - Stewart was signed from Ayr United for £30,000 in October 1973 - he had just two runs spanning three seasons in the first team, in 1975 and 1977, when Harvey was injured. Yet there was never any sense of Stewart being a second-rate goalkeeper, for his bravery and splendid reflexes made him an admirable deputy. Stewart's performances made sufficient impression for him to be called up by Scotland in 1977 and, during his sole international match against East Germany, he saved a penalty.

Stewart approached games in an unruffled collected manner - in stark contrast to the acute tension that gripped Gary Sprake and made him sick before matches - and, for a player who had to learn a great deal quickly, impressed colleagues with his coolness in tense situations. Having tasted action at the highest level - Stewart made some heroic contributions in the latter stages of Leeds' march to the European Cup Final in 1975, not least during the semi-final in Barcelona - it was unsurprising that despite his patience he became disenchanted playing second fiddle to Harvey. In 1978, he transferred to West Bromwich Albion - for whom he did not play in the league - and thence to Swansea City in 1980.

BORN: Glasgow 11.3.47.
GAMES: 74. GOALS: 0
HONOURS: 1 Scotland Cap 1978.
OTHER CLUBS: Ayr United 67/8-73/4; West Bromwich Albion (0, 0);
Swansea City 79/80-80/1 (57, 0).

1973/74 - 1978/79

GORDON McQUEEN

The tall blond Gordon McQueen, looking like some Nordic god, was probably the most impressive physical specimen to pull on a Leeds United shirt. At six feet three and a half, it was easy to imagine McQueen in his youthful footballing life as a goalkeeper - which he was - but less so as winger - which also he was. As a centre-half, and replacement for Jack Charlton, he modelled well for the part.

Among the clubs with which Ayrshire-born McQueen failed to make the grade as a youngster were Liverpool and Glasgow Rangers. Instead of Anfield or Ibrox, he found himself playing in modest surroundings at St Mirren before Don Revie bought him in September 1972 for just £30,000.

With Charlton's retirement in 1973, Revie decided the 21-year-old McQueen was ready to be pitched into the first division. Surrounded by wily old hands such as Hunter, Madeley and Reaney to provide him with a detailed anatomy of any troublesome opponent, the transition was less traumatic for McQueen than it might have been. He obeyed Revie's dictum to play a simple no-frills game yet for a man of his height was surprisingly mobile; no mere gangling stopper. With McQueen's arrival as a first team regular coincided Leeds' record-breaking 29-match unbeaten run, some of the most fluid football the team ever produced, and a second League Championship.

Inevitably, McQueen showed unease in some early games. But he had much to offer with his aerial domination, the full-blooded effort he put into saving any dangerous situation and surging runs from the penalty area that could turn defence into attack. Like his team-mate and friend Joe Jordan, McQueen, in such exalted company, matured with astonishing speed. Fifteen months after he made his Leeds first team debut, McQueen won his first of 30 Scottish caps in June 1974. An Achilles tendon injury restricted McQueen's appearances for Leeds in 1975/6, when he was was badly missed, and in 1978 his ambition for greater things than Leeds could offer took him to Manchester United at a cost of £495,000.

BORN: Kilbirnie, Ayrshire, 26.6.52.
GAMES: 170 (1). GOALS: 19.
HONOURS: League Championship 73/4.
30 Scotland Caps 74-81.
OTHER CLUBS: St Mirren 71/2;
Manchester United 77/8-83/4 (172, 19);
Seiko FC, Hong Kong.
MANAGER: Airdrie 87/8-88/9.

1972/73 - 1977/78

JOHN McGOVERN

John McGovern deserved better than the wretched seven months he endured at Leeds which dislocated his career. However, the circumstances of his move from Derby to Elland Road were extraordinary: he was something of a pawn in new manager Brian Clough's determination to stamp his authority on Leeds United and uproot Don Revie's wilful old henchmen.

But the wilful old henchmen had just won the League Championship again. They were still good and they knew it.

McGovern was a neat, tidy, quite stylish midfielder who performed with great economy of effort, but that was never enough for the Elland Road crowd. When he arrived, Billy Bremner was suspended following his fracas with Kevin Keegan in the FA Charity Shield, but by no means finished. Johnny Giles was still buzzing. McGovern's four league appearances coincided with a stuttering start. As Clough's envoy, McGovern was a prime target for disgruntled Leeds fans.

When Clough was sacked and Bremner made a belated return, there was no future for McGovern at Leeds. His finest hours lay ahead of him, for, in February 1975, he followed his leader to Nottingham Forest and in a side that Clough was allowed to reconstruct, played with quiet authority as Forest won the League Championship, the League Cup, twice, and twice the European Cup. Not being good enough for Leeds had its compensations.

BORN: Montrose, 28.10.49. GAMES: 4. GOALS: 0.
OTHER CLUBS: Hartlepool United 65/6-68/9 (71, 5);
Derby County 68/9-73/4 (190, 16); Nottingham Forest 74/5-81/2 (253, 6); Bolton Wanderers 82/3-83/4 (16, 0).
PLAYER-MANAGER: Bolton Wanderers 82/3-84/5.

1974/75

JOHN O'HARE

John O'Hare, who came and went from Leeds in the same package as his team-mate John McGovern, also suffered from being labelled one of Brian Clough's men. Like McGovern, with whom he trod the same career path, O'Hare's best days were at Derby and Nottingham Forest either side of his seven months at Leeds, although during that time he might claim to have made marginally more impact: six league games as opposed to McGovern's four, and a goal.

Yet O'Hare impressed a number of his Leeds team-mates. He showed signs of leading the front-line well, with strength and determination, and a good eye for goal, even if he was not the keenest trainer on Leeds United's books. But when O'Hare was brought in, Leeds scarcely needed another front man of his kind with Joe Jordan on hand to maul opposing defences.

O'Hare, a Scotland international, was regarded as a good player but of insufficient calibre to displace any of the existing team. When he packed his bags with John McGovern and left for Nottingham, he could start again and, liberated from Elland Road, share in Forest's finest hours.

BORN: Renton, near Dumbarton, 24.9.46.
GAMES: 7. GOALS: 1.
HONOURS: 13 Scotland Caps 70-72.
OTHER CLUBS: Sunderland 64/6 (51, 14);
Derby County 67/8-73/4 (248, 65);
Nottingham Forest 74/5-79/80 (101, 14);
Dallas Tornados, USA (on loan) 77.

1974/75

DUNCAN McKENZIE

Duncan McKenzie had extravagant, almost freakish skills and athleticism but also, it seemed sometimes, an indifferent attitude to soccer. That he therefore became a favourite at Elland Road is perhaps surprising, especially as he had been signed by Brian Clough.

McKenzie was famed almost as much for his sideshows as his football; his ability to jump over cars and throw a golf ball the length of a pitch. But despite his air of feyness, when in the mood and well-served, McKenzie was an exciting, potent striker during his two seasons at Leeds. Yet he infuriated team-mates on days he chose to be a law unto himself and indulge in exhibitionism when more humdrum qualities were needed.

In 1975/6, established at number 9 as Allan Clarke's striking partner in a fairly settled side, the goals flowed: 16 in 39 league matches. Few of these were less than elegant, whether his delicate far post header in the home game against Newcastle or, a collector's item during Leeds' 4-0 rout of Leicester on December 27, where McKenzie, showing great elasticity and technique, stretched out, controlled the ball, then spun round before scoring with a crisp snap-shot. The bigger the game, the more likely he was to excel.

McKenzie left Leeds at the end of 1975/6, to roam around several clubs. Among the most articulate players of his generation, he has since worked as a newspaper columnist as well as becoming an after-dinner speaker.

BORN: Grimsby, 10.6.50. GAMES: 76 (5). GOALS: 30.
OTHER CLUBS: Nottingham Forest 69/70-73/4 (111, 41);
Mansfield Town (*on loan*) 69/70 and 72/3 (16, 10);
Anderlecht, Belgium, 76/7; Everton 76/7-77/8 (48, 14); Chelsea 78/9 (15, 4);
Blackburn Rovers 78/9-80/1 (74, 16); Tulsa Roughnecks, USA.

1974/75 - 1975/77

FRANK GRAY

Frank Gray, while less of an ornate footballing genius than his brother Eddie, showed such abundant youthful promise that around thirty clubs scrambled for his signature. As a schoolboy, Frank had idolised Glasgow Celtic but was wooed to Elland Road in 1971 - six years after Eddie - by Don Revie's artful persuasion.

Frank's career brought him a European Cup winners medal (with Nottingham Forest), and 32 international caps for Scotland yet leaves among some admirers a sense of talent unfulfilled. It was as if the younger Gray were so at ease with his ability he had little incentive to struggle for self-improvement and make the transition from being a very fine player into a great one.

The raw material was there. Nature was extravagant when bestowing gifts on the Gray brothers. Frank was fast, a superb passer of the ball, read the game with intuitive intelligence, was a cool taker of penalty kicks and generally played a simple but stylish game. Although his bias, like Eddie's, was for the left side, he played deeper. His assorted abilities gave him many options and though eventually he became a left-back, some believe he was a finer player in midfield.

Perhaps he did not always relish that burden. But there were times, when deployed at the centre of things, Frank Gray showed electrifying ability. Few who were there will forget a fourth round FA Cup tie at Birmingham in 1977, an intense crackling match in which he drove Leeds forward with boundless verve and energy to a 2-1 victory. Yet it was Nottingham Forest, a more coherent team when he joined them in July 1979, and particularly Scotland, who enjoyed the best of Frank Gray.

He had two spells at Leeds, the second came after he joined Nottingham Forest and harvested the honours his talents deserved. He finally left Elland Road for good in 1985 to join Sunderland, transferred by brother-manager Eddie. Whenever Frank came and went, it was without rancour; whenever he lost - as often happened in the dark early 80s - it seemed not quite to hurt enough. If, as an adjunct to his great natural gifts, Frank Gray had had the passion of a Bremner, a Collins or a Hunter, he might have been have been irresistible.

BORN: Glasgow, 27.10.54.
GAMES 396 (9). GOALS: 35.
HONOURS: 32 Scotland Caps 76-83.
OTHER CLUBS: Nottingham Forest 79/80-81/2 (81, 5);
Sunderland 85/6-88/9 (146, 8).
PLAYER-MANAGER: Darlington 89/90-91/2 (49, 7).

1973/74 - 1978/79 & 1981/82 - 1984/85

TONY CURRIE

When Tony Currie chose to flaunt his rippling skills he could stop Leeds fans looking to the glorious past and convince them the club might become reacquainted with great days. His signing from Sheffield United by Jimmy Armfield in summer 1976 looked like a declaration of ambitious intent. Giles had gone; Bremner would play just a handful more games. Enter a new man, with a different style but blessed with creative genius. The midfield kings were dead: long live the crown prince.

Yet for a player so central to everything, Currie sometimes lacked the fire and the fervour of his predecessors. His passing, shooting, and vision were the equal of anyone's and he cut the most impressive figure of any Leeds United midfielder when embarking on muscular runs before spraying the ball to colleagues with delectable accuracy. At times though, he played with a languor Don Revie would never have tolerated.

However, Currie was less of a soft touch than some critics believe. He had the strength and ability to win the ball for himself in some of the fiercest areas of midfield even though a scuffling, chivvying game was not to his taste. His preferred style was to throw defences into turmoil either by using his power and close control to run at them, or striking passes to colleagues that probed the weakest spots.

Tony Currie loved the big occasions. During his three seasons at Leeds, there were enough of these to coax out his full repertoire of talents. For every Leeds fan there are Currie vignettes to savour but also enthralling full-blooded performances such as those in the fourth round FA Cup tie at West Bromwich of February 1979, in a 3-3 draw of almost uncontainable excitement, and in a league match at Tottenham five weeks earlier where Currie bestrode the field with a dominance that suggested he could have locked up the match and slipped it into his back pocket whenever he chose.

Though he could strike the ball with fierce accuracy, Currie was never a prolific scorer. In the absence of quantity there was, of course, quality, such as his flamboyant showman's banana shot against Southampton during the 4-0 home win of November 1978. In all, Currie won 17 England caps, 11 while playing for Leeds, and while some critics feel he never fully exploited his brilliance, enough was seen to leave a sense of pleasure for what he gave rather than sorrow for a talent unfulfilled.

BORN: Edgware, London: 1.1.50.
GAMES: 124. GOALS: 16.
HONOURS: 17 England Caps 72-79.
OTHER CLUBS: Watford 67/8 (18, 9);
Sheffield United 67/8-75/6 (313, 55);
Queen's Park Rangers 79/80-82/3 (81, 5);
Torquay United 83/4 (9, 0).

1976/77 - 1979/80

EDDIE GRAY

Who was the most skilful player in Britain during the 1960s and 1970s? The media bandied about the name of George Best but Leeds fans knew of a man with a lower profile yet who had all Best's technical accomplishments. Of the brilliant players assembled by Don Revie, Eddie Gray was the most extravagantly gifted. When Revie and Leeds coach Syd Owen first saw him as a 15-year-old performing for Scotland schoolboys in 1963, they could hardly believe their eyes. Neither could a legion of other talent spotters, for Leeds were among around 30 clubs in hot pursuit of the Glaswegian teenager.

Yet despite the overtures of more glamorous clubs - including Celtic, the club of his boyhood dreams - it was the wily Revie who plucked Gray away from his secondary school and signed him. Gray made his debut against Sheffield Wednesday on New Year's Day 1966, a match in which he scored. But what should have been one of the great football careers of all time was blighted by injury.

From 1970 to 1975, Eddie Gray might have expected his skills on the left wing to have put the footballing world at his feet. Yet in all that time, he made just 82 league appearances. Had he been able to produce his enthralling dribbling skills regularly, an already magnificent side might have been almost invincible. For on form, the modest and diffident Gray was a miraculous sight. No-one who witnessed the 1970 Cup Final will forget his bravura exhibition of wing play, and the sight of Chelsea right-back David Webb turned inside out time after time as Gray, quite merciless for once, bore down on the Chelsea goal.

Some wingers on song might beat two or three opponents. When Eddie Gray was in the mood, he would make it five or six. With his distinctive loping run and shoulders hunched, he could thread a path through a mass of defenders - and score - as he did with such panache when playing for Scotland against Cyprus at Hampden in 1969 and for Leeds at Elland Road in a league match against Burnley in April 1970.

By the time Eddie Gray finally attained fitness and a more regular place in the side, the great team built by Don Revie was breaking up around him. In his latter years, he was converted to left-back; less speedy by then but always stylish and an intelligent reader of the game. When Gray was appointed player-manager of Leeds United in 1982, the team of elegant talented young players he tried to fashion was perhaps too soft for its own good. But undoubtedly it bore the hallmark of a master craftsman.

BORN: Glasgow 17.1.48.
Games: 559 (18). GOALS: 68.
HONOURS: League Championship 68/9, 73/4; FA Cup 71/2;
Inter Cities Fairs Cup 67/8; League Cup 67/8.
12 Scotland Caps 69-77.

1965/66 - 1983/84

DAVID McNIVEN

David McNiven's appearances in a white shirt were few but his sometimes theatrical goal-scoring interventions as a late substitute linger in the memory. A compact, stocky striker signed by Leeds as a junior in 1972, he made his debut in a League Cup match against Notts County in October 1975 and saw most of his first team action in 1976/7.

McNiven, a Scotsman who won three under-21 caps, was most effective playing in short concentrated bursts. He took to the field brimming with energy, ready to pounce on a crumb of a half chance in the penalty area. His darting nippy style seemed to catch tiring defences unawares, most notably Liverpool's, when his late goal in a 1-1 draw at Elland Road in October 1976 gave Leeds the least they deserved from a fine, fluid performance.

At only five feet six however, McNiven, despite his strength, was limited as a target man and with the return to fitness of Ray Hankin, he disappeared from the first team almost as suddenly as he had arrived. He was sold to Bradford City for £25,000 in February 1978.

BORN: Stonehouse, Lanarkshire 9.9.55.
GAMES: 16 (7). GOALS: 6.
OTHER CLUBS: Bradford City 77/8-82/3 (212, 64);
Blackpool 82/3-83/4 (49, 11);
Portland Timbers, USA, 84/5; Pittsburgh Spirit, USA, 84/5;
Halifax Town 84/5 (12, 4).

1975/76 - 1977/78

PETER HAMPTON.

Peter Hampton endured five years of reserve team football waiting for the famous old Leeds guard to fade away before he could claim a first team place. He was signed as a 17-year-old after leaving school in 1971, and like his predecessor at left-back Terry Cooper, was a converted winger. Hampton, having suffered two cartilage injuries as a teenager, recognised he had insufficient pace to make an impact up front.

Once given his chance by Jimmy Armfield in 1976/7 - Frank Gray was moved into midfield to accommodate him - Hampton showed himself worthy of the place he had coveted. He was a reliable quick-thinking defender, a crisp tackler, and while not a memorable passer of the ball, his distribution was generally adequate. Hampton does not linger in the memory for his attacking qualities but his handful of cherished goals includes a spectacular rasping left-foot shot from outside the penalty area that clinched Leeds' 2-1 home win over Burnley in April 1976.

Despite consistent displays in 1976-7, Hampton was supplanted by Frank Gray and Trevor Cherry at left-back. Unable to regain a regular first team place, he transferred to Stoke for £175,000 in August 1980 where he continued to give stout, honest performances.

BORN: Oldham, 12.9.54. GAMES: 76 (7). GOALS: 3.
OTHER CLUBS: Stoke City 80/1-83/4 (138, 4);
Burnley 84/5-86/7 (118, 2);
Rochdale 87/8 (19, 1);
Carlisle United 87/8 (12, 0).

1972/73 - 1979/80

BRIAN FLYNN

If some Leeds United fans hoped the diminutive Brian Flynn might replace Billy Bremner on the right side of midfield when he arrived from Burnley in November 1977, they were deluding themselves. It was tempting to make wishful comparisons: both were short, industrious players, fully committed to their trade. But whereas Bremner was a genius, a player of unsurpassable skill and vision, Flynn's talents were more mundane.

Still, he has moments to treasure from his career at Leeds - and his 66 appearances for Wales - and games of which he can be proud. His fierce rising shot from the edge of a crowded penalty area that brought Leeds victory at Manchester United during February 1981 would, in the eyes of some fans, be sufficient grounds for granting him the freedom of the Yorkshire city. However, Flynn's more typical game was to try to generate opportunities by buzzing and harrying in midfield.

He was more than a hustler though. Flynn had good control, a neat first touch and, when on form, was quick-witted enough to strike opportunist passes long and short that split opposition defences. But on his less good days, for all his huffing and puffing, he looked ineffectual and less potent without Tony Currie. It is not unusual for a player of Flynn's energetic style to be on a short fuse, or occasionally to mistime his tackles, and sometimes he became the centre of stormy battles on the pitch.

As Allan Clarke made fruitless experiments to try to stave off relegation, Flynn returned to Burnley on loan in March 1982, eventually rejoining his old club permanently at the end of the year. He saw out his career in the lower divisions, finally moving to Wrexham where he became manager.

BORN: Port Talbot, South Wales, 12.10.55. GAMES: 174 (3). GOALS: 11.
HONOURS: 66 Wales Caps 75-84.
OTHER CLUBS: Burnley 72/3-77/8, 81/2 *(on loan)*, 82/3-84/5 (202, 19); Cardiff City 84/5-85/6 (32, 0);
Doncaster Rovers 85/6 (27, 0); Bury 86/7 (19, 0); Wrexham 87/8-91/2 (98, 5).
MANAGER: Wrexham 89-

1977/78 - 1982/83

JOE JORDAN

The swiftness of Joe Jordan's ascent to become Mick Jones' heir at Elland Road took many by surprise. But even before it was apparent that by the end of the 1973/4 season Jones' much-battered knee would take no more punishment and force him out of the game, Jordan, signed in October 1970 for a mere £15,000 from Morton after being recommended to Don Revie by Bobby Collins, had made his mark at Elland Road. And on a few first division defenders.

Like Jones, Jordan was full of brave, direct running, but more inclined to become embroiled in fierce conflict. With his temper aroused - he had a fairly low flashpoint when the going was rough - Jordan, bearing down on his foe in search of retribution with a glowering toothless snarl, was an unnerving sight.

Many of his early appearances were made as substitute and sometimes Jordan found it hard to pick up the pace and mood of the game. But once given a run in the Leeds first team, Jordan devoured his opportunities, using his height and strength in the air to master many more experienced opponents, and direct telling passes with his head. His eagerness for possession and the ability to hold the ball under pressure helped open up gaps for his colleagues.

Fiery though he was, Jordan showed impressive composure under intense pressure. When in 1973/4, Leeds were grimly defending their 23 match unbeaten record from the start of the season, Jordan it was three minutes from time who received Lorimer's cross, steadied himself, then drove the ball home to rescue a cause that was seemingly lost.

Jordan's fierce style of play belied his diffident soft-spoken manner off the field. But despite his retaliatory blazes he showed considerable intelligence and maturity on the pitch. Within two years of making his Elland Road debut, Jordan won his first Scottish cap, as substitute against England, and in 1974 scored a thundering header against Czechoslovakia that took his country to the World Cup finals in West Germany. Jordan's departure, in 1978, from a declining Leeds team allowed him to enhance his career at Manchester United and AC Milan. The skills he subsequently learned as manager at Bristol City have helped re-establish Hearts as a force in Scottish football.

BORN: Carluke, Lanarkshire 15.12.51.
GAMES: 182 (38). GOALS: 48.
HONOURS: League Championship 73/4.
52 Scotland Caps 73-82.
OTHER CLUBS: Manchester United 77/8-80/1 (109, 37);
AC Milan, Italy, 81/2-82/3 (52, 12); Verona, Italy, 83/4 (12, 1);
Southampton 84/5-85/6 (48, 12);
Bristol City 86/7-88/9 (46, 8).
MANAGER: Bristol City 87/8-90/1; Hearts 90/1-.

1971/72 - 1977/78

CARL HARRIS

There were times when, as Carl Harris darted down the flanks and ran at defenders, he could cause as much panic among defences as any winger in the land. A former Welsh schoolboy international, he was signed in 1973 by Don Revie who - not for the first time - managed to woo back a promising young player who had returned to Wales feeling homesick.

Harris scored on his debut when coming on as substitute against Ipswich Town during the 2-1 home win in April 1975 and eventually replaced Peter Lorimer on the right wing. He was a speedy, direct player with an eye for goal but once established as a first team regular in the late 1970s and early 80s, found himself in a less able and consistent team than in the Revie days. For all his ability, some of Harris' own performances were wayward.

When in form, Harris on the right flank and Arthur Graham on the left could provide sparkling, if sometimes isolated entertainment. On a good day, the Harris style would be to make rapid ground down the right and provide dangerous crosses or powerful shots from the edge of the penalty area that flew towards goal. On a bad day, he appeared too easily discouraged, ineffectual, ill-attuned to the game, and gave away the ball too easily.

Eleven months after his debut, Harris was called up by Wales for the match against England and won 24 caps whilst with Leeds. After Leeds were relegated in 1982, he transferred to Charlton, where he showed good form before injuries interrupted his career.

BORN: Neath, South Wales, 3.11.56.
GAMES: 136 (40). GOALS: 29.
HONOURS: 24 Wales Caps 76-82.
OTHER CLUBS: Charlton Athletic 82/3-84/5 (76, 7); Bury 85/6-86/7 (38, 4);
Rochdale 87/8-88/9 (25, 3); Exeter City 88/9 (16, 1).

1974/75 - 1981/82

GWYN THOMAS

Leeds United have had many players more talented than Gwyn Thomas but he could match anyone for hustling endeavour. While his presence in the team may have evinced to some disgruntled supporters the club's great days were over and its horizons limited, others appreciated Thomas for his whole-hearted honesty and sometimes reckless socks-rolled-down approach to the game.

In nine years at Elland Road, Thomas played just a handful of first division games each season following his debut against Wolves in April 1975. In 1982, after Leeds were relegated, he was brought in regularly by Eddie Gray to fill assorted midfield and defensive positions.

Thomas' main strength was his fearless tackling and afterwards laying off the ball to team-mates; his principal weakness, giving the ball away through an ill-considered pass. A regular in 1982/3, he was sold to Barnsley for £40,000 as Eddie Gray continued his thankless experiment of trying to build a winning team on a straitened budget.

BORN: Swansea, 26.9.57.
GAMES: 92 (11) GOALS: 3.
OTHER CLUBS: Barnsley 83/4-89/90 (207, 17);
Hull City, 89/90-90/91 (22, 0).

1974/75 - 1983/84

BYRON STEVENSON

Byron Stevenson was among Don Revie's last signings, turning professional as a 17-year-old in September 1973. With the great side still near its peak, he did not hope easily to oust Norman Hunter, for whom originally he was considered a possible replacement, but might have expected a less peripheral role than the one he had during eight years at Elland Road.

Llanelli-born Stevenson was never quite commanding enough to be a natural first choice defender nor sufficently constructive with the ball to hold down a place in midfield. Injuries and suspension allowed him fitful appearances in the first team where his best, in a number of positions, was adequate rather than inspired.

Despite his limitations, Stevenson won 15 full caps for Wales though he may be best remembered at international level for a personal débâcle against Turkey in Izmir in 1979 when he was sent off for violent conduct and received a four year ban from UEFA. Stevenson left Leeds in March 1982 when Allan Clarke, desperate for goals to keep his side in the first division, traded him for Birmingham City's roving striker Frank Worthington.

BORN: Llanelli, South Wales, 7.12.56.
GAMES: 102 (8). GOALS: 5.
HONOURS: 15 Wales Caps 78-82.
OTHER CLUBS: Birmingham City 81/2-84/5 (74, 3);
Bristol Rovers 85/6 (31, 3).

1974/75 - 1981/82

ARTHUR GRAHAM

Arthur Graham was among the more constant and reassuring figures in a Leeds United side that was declining around him. If not a model of consistency, he was at least a player of first division and international calibre - Graham won 10 caps for Scotland - whose darting play on the left wing provided increasingly rare spectacles of excitement for Leeds fans.

Graham's career had a spectacular start. He won an FA Cup medal with Aberdeen in 1970 when just 17 and was a seasoned professional, with 230 appearances for the Scottish club when signed by Leeds for £125,000 in summer 1977. While not the most stylish player to grace the Leeds attack, many first division defences struggled to contain Graham's rapid scampering runs. He was adept at providing the ball most difficult to defend against, the ball cut back from near the by-line and, in lean times, was looked to as goal-scorer as well as provider. Graham was skilful and versatile enough to play on both flanks and through the middle.

With a less solid and creative midfield on which to lean, Graham often had to forage for the ball himself in deep positions. But he had the aggression to do so and the strength not to get knocked off the ball easily after winning possession. Graham turned in many industrious performances for Leeds and his willingness to shoot on sight after cutting in from the wings helped bring him 47 goals - including hat tricks against Valetta in the UEFA Cup and Birmingham and Wolves in the league - throughout all competitions.

Graham stayed just one more season after Leeds were relegated, and in the team's darker hours, his tendency to become disheartened showed itself on the pitch, although he was an excellent trainer and a popular, affable member of the Leeds team. In August 1983, he transferred to Manchester United for £50,000 where, with his morale restored, he produced several exhilarating performances.

BORN: Glasgow, 26.10.52.
GAMES: 259 (1). GOALS: 47. HONOURS:
10 Scotland Caps 78-81.
OTHER CLUBS: Aberdeen 69/70-76/7 (230, 32);
Manchester United 83/4-84/5 (37, 5);
Bradford City 85/6-86/7 (31, 2).

1977/78 - 1982/83

ALAN CURTIS

The poise and assurance with which Alan Curtis cruised past defenders towards the opposition penalty area suggested Leeds had secured a top-class striker, albeit that his provenance was third division Swansea. Signed in May 1979 for £400,000, a record for a player from the lower divisions, Curtis arrived in triumphant form, scoring two goals in his debut at Bristol City.

In early games, Curtis appeared a quick fluent player with a genuine striker's instinct for goal and the ability to provide chances through skilled passing or flicked headers. Alas for Leeds, injury and loss of form restricted his career at Elland Road to 18 months; for when Curtis returned to Swansea, then rising irresistibly through the divisions, he rediscovered his old élan. In all, he was capped 35 times for Wales.

In his brief time with Leeds, Curtis took part in some shockingly mediocre games. But he provided a handful of rich moments: his debut, of course, and, three months later, a glorious solo goal at Southampton when, in the dying minutes, he ran almost the length of the pitch to drive home a long-range shot that provided Leeds with a 2-1 victory. With such aplomb, Curtis brought delight to Leeds' mass of travelling supporters who had endured six months without an away win.

BORN: Ton Pentre, near Pontypridd 16.4.54.
GAMES: 35. GOALS: 6.
HONOURS: 35 Wales Caps 76-87.
OTHER CLUBS: Swansea City: 72/3-78/9, 80/1-83/4, 89/90 (372, 96);
Southampton 83/4-85/6 (50, 5); Stoke City (on loan) 85/6 (3, 0);
Cardiff City 86/7-88/9 (117, 10).

1979/80 - 1980/81

RAY HANKIN

The beginning of Ray Hankin's career at Elland Road was blighted by injury. A less determined striker than he may have found the excuse never to get going but once his knee fully recovered, Hankin set about pummelling defences in a quite fearsome manner.

He joined Leeds from Burnley for £172,000 but played just four matches - without scoring - in his first season, 1976/7. However, from day one of the following campaign with a goal at Newcastle, Hankin fairly crashed into the first division arena, scoring 20 league goals. He was tall, bulky, fearless and intimidating; and obstructing Hankin's 14 stone frame when he launched himself into dangerous places on a goal-scoring mission was not to be undertaken lightly. There were few less appealing prospects for defenders in the first few months of 1977/8 than confronting Hankin and Joe Jordan in tandem.

Hankin was notably well-served by Arthur Graham, whose supply of crosses from the left provided him with much fodder. As one might expect from someone six feet two, many goals came from his head though Hankin also had the beef to deliver a powerful shot. The following season, though less productive himself, Hankin established a fruitful partnership with John Hawley. Yet there were times when Hankin appeared more a clumsy bludgeoning instrument than a rapier. His first touch could be inept and he was also prone to getting involved in any rough stuff around him. Hankin left Leeds in March 1980 for the Canadian side Vancouver Whitecaps after the rapid ascent to the first team of teenager striker Terry Connor.

BORN: Wallsend, Tyneside, 2.2.56.
GAMES: 102 (1). GOALS: 36.
OTHER CLUBS: Burnley 72/3-76/7 (112, 37);
Vancouver Whitecaps, Canada, 80-81;
Middlesbrough 82/3-83/4 (21, 1); Peterborough United 83/4-84/5 (33, 8);
Wolverhampton Wanderers 84/5 (10, 1).

1976/77 - 1979/80

PAUL HART

It says much for Paul Hart's character that he prospered at Elland Road - and came even to be spoken of as a contender for the England centre-half spot - considering his calamitous arrival. An own-goal, assorted blunders, an air of seeming all at sea typified Hart's first few games for Leeds following his £300,000 transfer from Blackpool in March 1978.

Hart, though, stuck to learning his new job. Although more ungainly and with less pace than his predecessor Gordon McQueen, once acclimatised to the first division, Hart became a commanding defender. At six feet two, few strikers mastered him in the air and he was often a cool last line of defence when all around him was panic and disorder. The Hart style of clearance was unfancy though effective and the same could be said of his tackling for which the adjective rugged might have been invented.

At times Paul Hart was a little too determined strikers should not pass, and on several occasions he incurred the displeasure of the referee. But he was nothing if not brave and would carry on accepting the knocks that were a hazard of his trade without flinching. Hart was also a valuable piece of heavyweight artillery in attack when given room in which to launch himself at the ball.

His was a constant reassuring presence, even in Leeds' abortive struggle for first division survival. But after a season in division two, Paul Hart retained his ambition and appetite for top class football, and few were surprised when he transferred to Nottingham Forest in summer 1983.

BORN: Manchester 4.5.53. GAMES: 223. GOALS: 20.
OTHER CLUBS: Stockport County 70/1-72/3 (91, 5);
Blackpool 73/4-77/8 (143, 17); Nottingham Forest 83/4-84/5 (70, 1);
Sheffield Wednesday 85/6-86/7 (52, 2);
Birmingham City 86/7 (1, 0); Notts County 87/8 (23, 0).
MANAGER: Chesterfield, 88/9-90/1.

1977/78 - 1982/83

KEVIN HIRD

Watching Kevin Hird over the weeks of a season, it was hard to believe the same player could produce performances of such wildly variable quality, even allowing for the fact he was shunted between defence or midfield, wherever a gap arose. But perhaps the key to Hird's inconsistency was in the way he perceived himself. He had a diffident temperament and a low opinion of his own abilities; and was something of a puzzle to the Leeds management who saw him excel in training and display terrific enthusiasm.

Hird felt the burden of the £357,000 Leeds paid Blackburn Rovers for him in March 1979. His game was essentially a hard running one, whether at right-back or on the right side of midfield. Sometimes his head down and hunched shoulders posture did not make for accurate or inspired distribution, and he was prone to getting caught out of position. Yet Hird was a vigorous, honest player whose willingness to run could produce goal-scoring chances - as long as his crosses were up to the mark.

Hird could occasionally take opposing defences by surprise with the quality of his own finishing. It was strange a man who professed to doubt his fitness for the big-time should shoulder the burden of taking penalties but Kevin Hird did so dutifully, using his powerful shot to profitable effect. He was a good club man who soldiered on through some good times and the many bad times at Leeds before moving to Burnley in August 1984, where he concluded his league career.

BORN: Colne, Lancashire, 11.2.52.
GAMES: 181(19). GOALS: 21.
OTHER CLUBS: Blackburn Rovers 73/4-78/9 (132, 20);
Burnley 84/5-85/6 (83, 23).

1978/79 - 1983/84

GARY LIDDELL

WAYNE ENTWHISTLE

BILLY McGINLEY

GARY LIDDELL 1972/73-1974/75

Forward. BORN: Bannockburn, Stirlingshire, 27.8.54.
GAMES: 4 (2). GOALS: 1.
OTHER CLUBS: Grimsby Town 76/7-80/1 (105, 24);
Hearts 80/1 (24, 6); Doncaster Rovers 81/2-82/3 (37, 4).

NEIL PARKER 1977/78

Left-back. BORN: Blackburn, 19.10.57. GAMES: 0 (1). GOALS: 0.

JIMMY (SEAN) O'NEILL

1973/74. Full-back. BORN: Belfast, 24.2.52.
GAMES: 0 (3). GOALS: 0
OTHER CLUBS: Chesterfield 74/5-83/4 (358, 5).

JIMMY MANN 1971/72-1973/74

Forward/midfield. BORN: Goole, Yorkshire, 15.12.52.
GAMES: 4 (1). GOALS: 0.
OTHER CLUBS: Bristol City 74/5-81/2 (231, 31); Barnsley 81/2-
82/3 (15, 0); Scunthorpe United 82/3 (2, 0);
Doncaster Rovers 82/3 (13, 0).

GLAN LETHERAN 1973/74-1974/75

Goalkeeper. BORN: Llanelli, 1.5.56 GAMES: 1 (1). GOALS: 0.
OTHER CLUBS: Scunthorpe United (on loan) 76/77 (27, 0);
Chesterfield 77/78-79/80 (63, 0); Swansea City 79/80 (21, 0).

BILLY McGHIE 1976/77

Forward. BORN: Lanark, 19.1.58. GAMES: 2. GOALS: 1.
OTHER CLUBS: York City 79/80-81/82 (43, 1).

BILLY McGINLEY 1972/73-1973/74

Midfield. BORN: Dumfries, Scotland, 12.11.54.
GAMES: 0 (2). GOALS: 0. OTHER CLUBS: Huddersfield Town
74/5 (15, 1); 75/6-76/7 (60, 11); Crewe Alexandra 77/8 (38, 2).

WAYNE ENTWISTLE 1979/80

Centre-forward. BORN: Bury, 6.8.58. GAMES: 7 (5). GOALS: 2.
OTHER CLUBS: Bury 76/7-77/8, 83/4-84/5, 88/9 (116, 39);
Sunderland 77/8-79/80 (45, 12); Blackpool 80/1-81/2 (32, 6);
Crewe Alexandra 81/2 (11, 0); Wimbledon 82/3 (9, 3);
Carlisle United 85/6 (9, 2); Bolton Wanderers 85/6 (8, 0);
Burnley (on loan) 86/7 (8, 2); Stockport County 86/7-87/8 (49, 8);
Wigan Athletic 88/9 (29, 6); Hartlepool United 89/90 (2, 0).

NEIL PARKER

JIMMY MANN

GLAN LETHERAN

BILLY McGHIE

NEIL FIRM

JOHN McGOLDRICK

STEVE BALCOMBE

TONY ARINS

NEIL FIRM 1979/80-1981/82

Centre-half. BORN: Bradford, 12.1.58.
GAMES: 11 (1). GOALS: (0).
OTHER CLUBS: Oldham Athletic *(on loan)* 81/2 (9, 0);
Peterborough United 82/3-85/6 (72, 3).

DAVID WHYTE 1976/77

Midfield. BORN: Dunfermline, 2.3.59.
GAMES: 1 (1). GOALS: 0.

JOHN McGOLDRICK 1983/84

Right-back. BORN: Coatbridge, Lanarkshire, 23.9.63.
GAMES: 12. GOALS: 0.

ROGER ELI 1984/85-1985/86

Midfield. BORN: Bradford, 11.9.65. GAMES: 1 (1). GOALS: 0.
OTHER CLUBS: Wolverhampton Wanderers 85/6-86/7 (18, 0);
Crewe Alexandra 87/8-88/9 (27, 1); York City 88/9 (4, 1);
Bury 88/9 (2, 0); Burnley 89/90- (58, 19).

STEVE BALCOMBE 1981/82

Centre-forward. BORN: Bangor, North Wales, 2.9.61.
GAMES: 2. GOALS: 1. OTHER CLUBS: Home Farm, Dundalk,
Shamrock Rovers, Oaklands, (all Ireland).

PHIL HUGHES 1983/84-1984/85

Goalkeeper. BORN: Manchester, 19.11.64.
GAMES: 7. GOALS: 0. HONOURS: 3 Northern Ireland Caps, 87.
OTHER CLUBS: Bury 85/6-87/8 (80, 0); Wigan Athletic 87/8-
91/2 (99, 0); Scarborough *(on loan)* 91/2 (13, 0).

TONY ARINS 1981/82

Wing-half. BORN: Chesterfield, 26.10.58.
GAMES: 0 (1). GOALS: 0.
OTHER CLUBS: Burnley 78/9-79/80 (29, 2);
Scunthorpe United 81/2 (20, 1).

TONY BROWN 1982/83-1984/85

Centre-half. BORN: Bradford, 17.9.58. GAMES: 24. GOALS: 1.
OTHER CLUBS: Doncaster Rovers 84/5-86/7 (52, 2);
Scunthorpe United 86/7 (54, 2); Rochdale 89/90- (110, 0).

DAVID WHYTE

ROGER ELI

PHIL HUGHES

TONY BROWN

DEREK PARLANE

Whether it was something in the air at Elland Road, poor quality of service or whatever, the sharpness Derek Parlane showed over eight seasons at Ibrox deserted him all too often after Jimmy Adamson paid £200,000 in March 1980 to bring him to Leeds.

Perhaps a big match was needed to bestir Parlane. For while in many games he appeared sluggish and uninterested, there were occasional glimpses of form that made him look a bargain. In the final home game of 1979/80 against Manchester United, the prospect of denying the old enemy the League Championship galvanised a hitherto moderate-looking Leeds team; and Parlane's contribution was electrifying, from the confident goal he swept in early on, to his sharp running and adroit control that unnerved the Manchester defence throughout.

Such good days were rare and his goals were sparse. The seasons that followed were lean and in 1981/2, Parlane showed little fancy for a battle against relegation. Second division life at Maine Road, however, seemed to suit him better, albeit briefly. Having gone to Manchester City on a free transfer in August 1983, Parlane responded with a glut of goals. For Leeds fans, it must have seemed quite perverse that within weeks of changing his colours Parlane scored one of them at Elland Road to help inflict a 2-1 defeat on his old club.

BORN: Helensburgh, Dunbartonshire, 5.5.53. GAMES: 48 (5) GOALS 10.
HONOURS: 12 Scotland Caps 73-77.
OTHER CLUBS: Glasgow Rangers 69/70-79/80 (200,80);
Bulova, Hong Kong, 82/3; Manchester City 83/4-84/5 (48, 20); Swansea City 84/5 (21, 3);
North Shore FC, Hong Kong, 85/6; Racing Jet, Belgium, 86/7;
Rochdale 86/7-87/8 (42, 10); Airdrie 87/8 (9, 4).

1979/80 - 1982/83

TERRY CONNOR

By 1979, the great Leeds United side had disintegrated and Elland Road was a forlorn place for the dwindling number of supporters who yearned for new heroes. The first division home game against West Bromwich on November 17 had attracted only 17,000 fans and was spluttering along at 0-0 when 17-year-old Terry Connor took the field as substitute and burst through to score the winning goal.

Such is the stuff of dreams. The young black schoolboy from Leeds had made such a vivid start that he retained the number 9 shirt for the next eighteen matches. In that time he scored five goals and impressed everyone with his strength, speed, eye for goal, and the cool head normally found in a much more mature striker.

Premature and somewhat absurd claims were made for Connor, not least on the electronic scoreboard at Elland Road which on one occasion proclaimed him as Leeds' own Pele. Several journalists hurried to call him great. He was not, yet he did have immense promise and was wise enough not to swallow all the extravagant laudatory nonsense.

But Connor was playing in a team without the power and authority of its predecessors. After an early flush of promise, he went nine months without scoring; but then no-one else was getting goals regularly as Leeds muddled along in mid-table. With the collective decline in the team's form, Terry Connor lost his confidence and touch, though never his willingness to forage up front even in the least promising circumstances. When the club was relegated to the second division in 1982, he left for Brighton the following spring in a swap deal that brought Andy Ritchie to Leeds.

Many supporters had a sense of regret and lingering memories of Connor's vibrant first season; of a considerable talent that had lost its way through no real fault of the player. If only for a short while, Terry Connor brought colour and excitement to Leeds United when both commodities had been in pitifully short supply.

BORN: Leeds 9.11.62.
GAMES: 93 (15). GOALS: 22.
OTHER CLUBS: Brighton 82/3-86/7 (156, 51);
Portsmouth 87/8-89/90 (48, 12);
Swansea City 89/90-91/2 (38, 6);
Bristol City 91/2 (11, 1).

1979/80 - 1982/83

ALEX SABELLA

With memories still fresh of Argentina's swaggering success in the 1978 World Cup finals, the prospect of Alex Sabella coming to Elland Road was relished by Leeds fans. Though not a member of the victorious Argentinian team, Sabella's reputation as a midfielder of effervescent skill, based on some fine performances at Sheffield United, preceded him.

Since the departure of Tony Currie, the Leeds midfield was in desperate need of inspiration. Jimmy Adamson paid his Yorkshire rivals £400,000 for Sabella in August 1980, as if to emphasise that Leeds still aspired to compete with the best and would make a colourful splash when needed. The previous season, supporters had endured too many grey, listless performances.

It would have taken more than Sabella to effect the transformation Leeds fans were demanding. Jimmy Adamson was sacked within a month of Sabella's arrival and the Argentinian was never a favourite of Allan Clarke. Yet there were times when Sabella shone; where his remarkable ball control and accurate passing stood out. Sabella was an excellent runner with the ball in tight areas, if not over long distances, with a keen awareness of what others were doing around him.

Some team-mates considered Sabella a brilliant player who had the misfortune to be in the wrong place at the wrong time. He was a popular figure who worked and trained hard, who enjoyed his football but whose career in England evaporated within months of joining Leeds. It took a return to Argentina in January 1982 for Sabella to recover his form and, after joining Estudiantes for £120,000, to make his breakthrough into the national team.

BORN: Buenos Aires 5.11.54.
GAMES: 26 (1). GOALS: 2.
OTHER CLUBS: River Plate, Argentina;
Sheffield United 78/9-79/80 (76, 8),
Estudiantes, Argentina.

1980/81

JOHN HAWLEY

It is hard to ask more of a striker than that he scores 16 first division goals in 32 league outings, particularly when he costs only £80,000. Such was the dividend ex-Hull City forward John Hawley yielded in his one season at Elland Road. Why, with such a track record, he should have then been sold to Sunderland in a player plus cash deal that brought Wayne Entwistle, mystified many at Leeds.

Signing Hawley in May 1978 was among Jimmy Armfield's last acts before being sacked. Hawley was sold by Jimmy Adamson after it appeared his partnership with Ray Hankin had solved Leeds' scoring problems - 70 goals were scored during a season in which they finished fifth. Hawley practised his trade in a businesslike unfancy way. He was mobile, persistent, good in the air and cool-headed. Among his goals to savour was one at Anfield in November 1978 when he showed great composure as he bore down towards the Kop end before planting the ball firmly past Ray Clemence.

When transferred to Sunderland, Hawley, who also helped run his family's antiques business in Hull, continued to score freely in his limited appearances. Meanwhile, Leeds, lacking his services, scored just 46 goals the following season. Hawley had left behind him the first signs of famine at Elland Road.

BORN: Withernsea, Yorkshire, 8.5.54.
GAMES: 39 (3). GOALS: 17.
OTHER CLUBS: Hull City 72/3-77/8, (on loan) 82/3 (117, 23);
Sunderland 79/80-81/2 (25, 11); Arsenal 81/2-82/3 (20, 3);
Orient (on loan) 82/3 (4, 1); Happy Valley FC, Hong Kong, 83;
Bradford City 83/4-84/5 (67, 28); Scunthorpe United 85/6 (21, 7).

1978/79 - 1979/80

JEFF CHANDLER

The turmoil around him at Elland Road did nothing to enhance Jeff Chandler's career prospects after a £100,000 move to Elland Road from Blackpool in September 1979. He was imported to Leeds when loss of form and injuries to players made it seem there were no certainties at his new club.

Chandler, a left-sided midfield player, spent more time out of the first team than in it during his two years at Leeds. Yet when picked, he turned in some good performances. His penetrating runs and subtle passes were a feature of a rare Leeds win at Southampton in October 1979 which had as its topping Alan Curtis' exhilarating solo goal.

It was clear, however, Chandler did not feature in Allan Clarke's future plans and, having made only one first team appearance in the previous six months, he was sold to Bolton Wanderers in October 1981. There, for Chandler at least, life was more settled and he made more than 150 league appearances for the Burnden Park club.

BORN: London 19.6.59.
GAMES: 23 (5). GOALS: 2.
HONOURS: 2 Republic of Ireland Caps 80.
OTHER CLUBS: Blackpool 76/7-79/80 (37, 7);
Bolton Wanderers 81/2-84/5, 87/8-88/9 (181, 40);
Derby County 85/6-86/7 (46, 10);
Mansfield Town (on loan) 86/7 (6, 0);
Cardiff City 89/90-90/1 (25, 0).

1979/80 - 1980/81

PETER BARNES

Never has the purchase of any big name player been more cursed by Leeds fans than that of Peter Barnes whose reputation rests largely on one or two incandescent seasons at Manchester City. He was the wrong player at the wrong time and, costing £930,000, shockingly dear for a club sliding into debt as attendances slumped.

There were times, precious few, when Barnes treated Leeds fans to some wondrous wing-play; surging weaving runs that turned defenders inside out: skills so fine they seemed designed to mock more mundane players. But alas for Leeds, he appeared to cast himself in the role of expensive luxury. When sweat was needed, Barnes tended to make his excuses and leave. And why, cried Leeds supporters, when he did make such swift and thrilling progress down the left, did Barnes then so often centre the ball into the crowd behind the goal?

At times, Peter Barnes blamed the rest of the world for his shortcomings, not least coaches, whom he accused of exhorting players to become workhorses, heedless of their special talents. In practice, this meant Barnes required spoon-feeding by a less than brilliant midfield. He might dazzle for five minutes, then attach himself to an opposing defender and lament the deficiencies of his colleagues for not receiving the ball.

Amid the exasperating inconsistency were a few whole games of near-genius, notably a virtuoso performance when Leeds, destined for relegation, astounded everyone by winning 4-1 at Aston Villa who a month later were to win the European Cup. But the Peter Barnes experience at Leeds, when he dreamed of regaining his England slot while unable to command a first team place, is one both player and club would prefer to forget.

BORN: Manchester 10.6.57. GAMES: 62 (2). GOALS: 6.
HONOURS: 22 England Caps 78-82.
OTHER CLUBS: Manchester City 74/5-78/9, 86/7 (123, 15); West Bromwich Albion 79/80-80/81 (77, 23);
Real Betis, Spain, *(on loan)* 82/3-83/4; Coventry City 84/5 (18, 2); Manchester United 85/6-86/7 (20, 2);
Hull City 87/8 (11, 0); Bolton Wanderers *(on loan)* 87/8, 88/9 (5, 0); Port Vale *(on loan)* 87/8 (3, 0); Farense, Portugal;
Sunderland 88/9 (1, 0); Melbourne City, Australia.

1981/82 - 1983/84

KENNY BURNS

Perhaps Brian Clough realised Kenny Burns, though only 28, was past his best when he allowed Allan Clarke to bring him to Leeds in October 1981 for £400,000. Three years earlier, Burns had been voted Footballer of the Year having been switched to defence from his earlier role, at Birmingham, as a somewhat fearsome but effective striker. At Nottingham Forest, he had been the keystone of a structured, disciplined team.

But in his new environment, there was not the same strength and order around him. When Burns arrived, the Leeds defence had been leaking two goals a game. He was however, often deployed in midfield, to stiffen a team unsettled by injuries and low in confidence. It would have taken a player of exceptional calibre and character to revive Leeds' fortunes; and to his own and everyone's disappointment, Burns accompanied Leeds into division two.

Deprived of the exposure and privileges first division football had bestowed upon him, Burns too often played as if his heart were not in the game. Yet when in the mood, he could stir himself to give glimpses of his old indomitable form. While not the fastest player, he was a superb tackler and when he went up to head a ball, few could stop him winning it. One of his finest performances was against Newcastle United in the 1982/3 League Cup, a game on which Burns stamped his old authority, giving Kevin Keegan scarcely a kick. But with Leeds and Burns showing inconsistency and insufficient class to return to division one at the first attempt, it was unsurprising the player grew restless. In March 1983 he was loaned to Derby County for whom he signed permanently the following season before roaming around a clutch of other clubs in and outside the English league.

BORN: Glasgow 23.9.53. GAMES: 64 (2). GOALS: 4.
HONOURS: 20 Scotland Caps 1974–81.
OTHER CLUBS: Birmingham City 71/2-76/7 (170, 45);
Nottingham Forest 77/8-81/2 (137, 13);
Derby County *(on loan)* 82/3, 83/4-84/5 (38, 2); Notts County *(on loan)* 84/5 (2, 0);
Barnsley 85/6 (22, 0).

1981/82 - 1983/84

KEITH PARKINSON

If Keith Parkinson's ability had matched his commitment, he could have been a formidable central defender at Leeds. In some ways he was effective, being tall, strong in the air and hard to knock off the ball. No-one could ever fault him for lack of effort when he managed to get a game.

His appearances were sporadic, for Parkinson was never destined to be a first choice centre-half. He spent almost ten years at Elland Road hoping for the best but lived in the shadows first of Gordon McQueen and then Paul Hart. Any development Parkinson might have made was further hampered by injuries. On the field, his lack of pace was apparent and he was also rather immobile, sometimes unable to turn quickly enough to keep tabs on tricky opponents.

Parkinson had signed professional forms in 1973 and it was not until December 1982 he finally left Leeds to join Doncaster Rovers as a non-contract player. He later joined the police force.

BORN: Preston 28.1.56.
GAMES: 32 (6). GOALS: 0.
OTHER CLUBS: Hull City *(on loan)* 81/2 (1, 0);
Doncaster Rovers 81/2 (5, 0).

1975/76 - 1980/81

BRIAN GREENHOFF

Coming from Manchester United, Brian Greenhoff needed to produce more than a player from elsewhere if he were to endear himself to the Leeds fans - even though some had fond memories of his older brother Jimmy. At Old Trafford, Greenhoff had looked good: a mobile versatile player, supported by fine footballers buzzing around him, whether in defence or midfield. He was still only 26 and an established international when Jimmy Adamson paid £350,000 for him in August 1979.

But injuries at Leeds brought a premature end to Greenhoff's career. Hamstring strains and knee problems blighted his early days though he managed to shrug these off and regain some consistency in 1980/1 when Allan Clarke moved him to right-back as part of a relatively firm and settled defence alongside Paul Hart, Eddie Gray amd Trevor Cherry. Briefly, Greenhoff could feel at home and display the composure and positional sense that brought him 18 England caps.

But the following season - which was to be Leeds' last in first division football for eight years - injuries again intervened to end the unfortunate Greenhoff's troubled stay at Elland Road. By 1983, he had joined his brother Jimmy at Rochdale to finish a league career that promised much more than it yielded.

BORN: Barnsley 24.4.53.
GAMES: 74 (4). GOALS: 1.
HONOURS: 18 England Caps 76-80.
OTHER CLUBS: Manchester United 73/4-78/9 (221, 13);
Rochdale 82/3-83/4 (16, 0).

1979/80 - 1981/82

AIDAN BUTTERWORTH

It is a rare footballer who breaks into the first division aged 19, but who then decides by his early twenties that he is indifferent towards a career in the professional game. Such was Aidan Butterworth, who showed quickness and an eye for goal when given a regular run in 1982/3 during Leeds' first season after relegation, in which he finished top scorer with 11 league goals.

By then, the Leeds attack was the bluntest of instruments - no-one else scored more than five times in the league - and it was apparent the Butterworth-Connor partnership was too lightweight and inexperienced to trouble defences regularly. Yet Butterworth's speed alone could be dangerous and markers neglected him at their peril.

It was with reluctance that in March 1983 Eddie Gray, seeking a more seasoned striker, decided to trade Terry Connor for Brighton's Andy Ritchie but this partnership with Butterworth was, if anything, even more impotent. Meanwhile the phlegmatic Butterworth was showing increasing interest in physical education. After the end of 1983/4, during which once more the Leeds strikers toiled to no great effect, Butterworth renounced professional football and left for college. He did, however, reappear with Doncaster Rovers before dropping out of league football in 1987.

BORN: Leeds 7.11.61.
GAMES: 64 (10). GOALS: 17.
OTHER CLUBS: Doncaster Rovers 84/5-85/6 (50, 5).

1980/81 - 1983/84

GARY HAMSON

The tale of Gary Hamson's footballing life is a sad one of promise and courage being thwarted by injury. When he was signed by Leeds from Sheffield United for £140,0000 in July 1979, there were high hopes the 20-year-old Hamson would be an invigorating presence in midfield or, if needed, in defence.

There were times Hamson showed signs of fulfilling his promise. His energy seemed inexhaustible and he tackled with gusto - too much for his own good sometimes. Along with Hamson's considerable bravery, passing ability and shooting power, there lay also a temperamental streak that drew him into needless feuds on the pitch and earned him a nine-match suspension in February 1981.

The knee injury he sustained in the final match of 1981/2 at West Bromwich was overshadowed by the riotous accompaniment to a defeat that banished Leeds to the second division. Hamson missed all the following season save for a fourth round FA Cup tie at Arsenal. When eventually fit to return to the first team, Hamson settled in at left back where, though he was solid enough, his edge and pace had gone and he was no longer the eye-catching potential star he once had been.

BORN: Nottingham 24.9.59.
GAMES: 141 (10). GOALS: 4.
OTHER CLUBS: Sheffield United 76/8 (108, 8);
Bristol City 86/7 (12, 2);
Port Vale 86/7-87/8 (38, 3).

1979/80 - 1985/86

JOHN LUKIC

John Lukic began his footballing life as a rising talent in a declining Leeds United side and returned to Elland Road seven years later as the finished article, a giant among goalkeepers on whom it would be almost impossible to improve. Of Yugoslavian parentage, he was born in Chesterfield, birthplace of Gordon Banks, one of the most distinguished goalkeepers in English football history, and spotted by Leeds when playing for Derbyshire schools.

At six feet four, though lean of frame, Lukic cut an authoritative figure at once. After serving his apprenticeship, Lukic made his league debut for Leeds United in October 1979 at Brighton, two months before his nineteenth birthday, replacing David Harvey. Few would have guessed that match, a 0-0 draw, was to mark the start of 146 consecutive league appearances for Leeds.

John Lukic quickly displayed his completeness. Playing behind a team which, over those 146 matches was often brittle and short of confidence, he appeared agile, brave, athletic and remarkably mature: he conveyed a sense of having arrived at the top almost at once. Leeds United's descent into the second division in 1982 may be attributed to deficiencies beyond the defence. Lukic meanwhile, who had already won youth and England under 21 caps, was on the verge of full international honours. That more than ten years later he has yet to play a senior match for his country mystifies many in the game.

His talent made him hunger for a future the second division could not offer. When in March 1983 he asked Eddie Gray for a transfer, Lukic was promptly dropped. That summer, he departed for Arsenal where he was an immediate and enduring success; all confidence and coolness. (Lukic becomes a taciturn introvert before any important match yet usually remains unruffled during the action.) His future at Highbury seemed assured until he became reacquainted with David Seaman, the apprentice goalkeeper whose hopes he had thwarted at Leeds. Now, ten years on, as he arrived at Arsenal from Queen's Park Rangers, Seaman was widely considered the finest goalkeeper in the land.

But the undemonstrative Lukic knew he was too good to play second fiddle to anyone. Meanwhile, his old club, newly promoted to the first division was thinking big again. When Lukic decided he must leave, Howard Wilkinson eagerly disbursed the £1 million needed to bring him home. A player of international calibre was back where his fans felt he belonged, his reactions and anticipation as keen as ever, complete with monstrous kick and a sometimes unnerving penchant for dribbling the ball upfield in his efforts to urge on the attack.

BORN: Chesterfield 11.12.60.
GAMES: 263. GOALS: 0.
HONOURS: League Championship 91/2.
OTHER CLUBS: Arsenal 83/4-89/90 (223, 0).

1978/79 - 1982/83 & 1990/91-

Perhaps it was asking too much of Frank Worthington to be Leeds United's saviour. But the Elland Road crowd, which had a soft-spot for the gifted showman, loved him. Worthington at least brought some colour to a pallid side that was losing ground in the dog-fight at the basement of division one.

Worthington, with four clubs already behind him, arrived from Birmingham City, traded off for Byron Stevenson as Leeds desperately sought goals. It was one of Allan Clarke's more imaginative moves, albeit one born of desperation. In 17 games, his new 33-year-old striker scored nine goals but these were not enough to keep Leeds up. All too soon, the itinerant Worthington transferred his talents elsewhere.

Leeds fans saw enough of his skills for his departure to be mourned. Despite his seemingly indolent character, Worthington was a striker equipped with almost every talent: superb control, the strength to shield the ball and hold up play, the wit to cause confusion and uncertainty in defences by deft flicks that switched the direction of attack, the ability to score goals from any angle, in any fashion, with almost cocky assurance.

Worthington's earlier clubs, Huddersfield, and especially Leicester had enjoyed the best fruit of his talents but he was still a fine if fading player by the time he arrived at Leeds. Within Frank Worthington lay the raw material of greatness but he was perhaps too lacking in seriousness to milk his talent for its full worth.

BORN: Halifax 23.11.48. GAMES: 35. GOALS: 15.
HONOURS: 8 England Caps 74-75.
OTHER CLUBS: Huddersfield Town 66/7-71/2 (171, 42); Leicester City 72/3-77/8 (210, 72);
Bolton Wanderers 77/8-79/80 (84, 35); Birmingham City 79/80-81/82 (75, 30); Sunderland 82/3 (19, 2);
Southampton 83/4 (34, 4); Brighton 84/5 (31, 7); Tranmere 85/6 (42, 18);
Preston North End 86/7 (23, 3); Stockport (on loan) 87/8 (19, 6).

1981/82 - 1982/83

DENIS IRWIN

The performances of Denis Irwin did not always catch the eye as do those of players with more flamboyant skills. Often it might be after the match was over you realised the young Irish right-back had, once again, contained the opposition left-winger and rarely been beaten for pace.

Although quiet and usually undemonstrative, Irwin had an inner confidence. He trained hard and it was clear to Eddie Gray and Jimmy Lumsden they had unearthed another young player steady enough for the first division. Inevitably, Irwin sometimes made mistakes but usually he played a tidy sound game, as well as enhancing the attack with the high standard of crosses he supplied after venturing upfield.

Irwin made his debut on a dismal night for Leeds, the 4-2 FA Cup third round defeat at Scunthorpe in January 1984. Within three months, he took over the number 2 shirt and the following season, which promised much for Leeds, missed only one match. But when Eddie Gray was sacked in October 1985, the turbulence that accompanied Billy Bremner's arrival unsettled him and by the end of the season, Irwin was transferred to Oldham Athletic for £60,000; if not quite given away, then sold very cheaply. Irwin distinguished himself during four seasons at Oldham who, when selling him to Manchester United for £650,000 a stronger, wiser player, realised something like his true value.

BORN: Cork, Ireland, 31.10.65. GAMES: 80. GOALS: 1.
HONOURS: 13 Republic of Ireland Caps 91-92.
OTHER CLUBS: Oldham Athletic 85/6-89/90 (167, 4);
Manchester United 90/1 (72, 3).

1983/84 - 1985/86

ANDY LINIGHAN

When in July 1990, Arsenal paid Norwich £1.3 million for the former Leeds defender Andy Linighan, it looked as if another of Eddie Gray's school, bought and sold cheaply, was heading for the top having made, in the transitional years, a handsome profit for other clubs. But despite Linighan's achievements, the story is less straightforward. A lack of confidence, detectable at Elland Road in his early career, has arrested his development.

At six feet four, Andy Linighan, bought by Eddie Gray from Hartlepool for £20,000, could hardly fail to command the air. In practice games and for real, he also showed a neatness on the ball for such a tall man, a bonus that came as an agreeable surprise to the Leeds management.

Linighan made his debut against Notts County in the first match of 1984/5 and, that season, was an ever-present in Eddie Gray's stable and attractive team. But in a way, Linighan's deficiencies, a reluctance to badger colleagues and impose his presence on matches, embodied the principal defect in a side which, had it been a little sterner, might have made it to division one.
The following season, Billy Bremner looked to hardened professionals to help get Leeds up. In February 1986, Linighan was sold to Oldham Athletic - the path of talented young Leeds old boys to Boundary Park was to become a well-trodden one - and was replaced the following month by Brendan Ormsby.

BORN: Hartlepool 18.6.62. GAMES: 74. GOALS: 4.
OTHER CLUBS: Hartlepool United 80/1-83/4 (110, 4);
Oldham Athletic 85/6-87/8 (87, 6);
Norwich City 87/8-89/90 (86, 8); Arsenal 90/1 - (25, 0).

1984/85 - 1985/86

MARTIN DICKINSON

Although pitched into the Leeds United side for his first few games in 1980 when just turned 17, Martin Dickinson saw most of his action for Leeds when under Eddie Gray's management. He was among a crop of home-grown youngsters - of very variable talents - from which Gray sought to build a team under severe financial constraints.

Dickinson was an auxiliary defender-cum-midfield man who gave his all for Leeds. His greatest asset was his speed; in a race for any long high ball knocked down the pitch, Dickinson was always the likely winner. But there were times, no doubt from sheer enthusiasm, he tried to do stylish things with the ball for which he was ill-equipped. Dickinson was an artisan, not an artist in the game.

After Eddie Gray was sacked in October 1985, Dickinson was among the first players to be moved on by Billy Bremner, sold to West Bromwich Albion for £40,000 in February 1986. He spent two years with the Midlands club before moving to Sheffield United but while there was involved in a car crash and sustained injuries that forced him to retire from the game.

BORN: Leeds 14.3.63. GAMES: 116 (2). GOALS: 2.
OTHER CLUBS: West Bromwich Albion 85/6-87/8 (50, 2);
Sheffield United 88/9 (1, 0).

1979/90 - 1985/86

JOHN DONNELLY

John Donnelly, a left-sided midfielder bought from Dumbarton in March 1983, was Eddie Gray's first signing and a source of puzzlement and exasperation to the Elland Road management. He had good skill and control, a powerful shot, and was one of the fittest players at the club. Yet only rarely did Donnelly's performances display these combined qualities.

Homesickness may have been partly to blame for his irresolute attitude to the game. Donnelly found being away from the Glasgow area hard to cope with. At times Donnelly's bosses felt his behaviour was that of someone who regarded football as a part-time occupation. Despite the lengths he went to keep fit, and that he rarely gave the ball away on the field, Gray and his assistant Jimmy Lumsden would have preferred some personal discipline as well.

By 1984, Donnelly drifted out of the Leeds first team and back to Glasgow to play for Partick Thistle. He later joined Dunfermline Athletic where, in 1988, after two years with the East End Park club, the management announced he was sacked after failing to report for duty.

BORN: Glasgow 8.3.61. GAMES: 40 (4). GOALS: 4.
OTHER CLUBS: Motherwell 78/9-79/80 (19, 2);
Dumbarton 80/1-82/3 (78, 17);
Partick Thistle 84/5-85/6 (39, 17);
Dunfermline Athletic 86/7-87/8 (34, 7).

1982/83 - 1984/85

ANDY WATSON

Andy Watson must have found coming to Leeds, after sharing many great intoxicating moments as a member of Alex Ferguson's triumphant Aberdeen team of the early 1980s, as sobering as being plunged into an icy bath. Morale at Elland Road was low, and Eddie Gray's team recruitment policy governed almost wholly by financial constraints.

Gray paid £60,000 for Watson hoping, perhaps, some of the glory of Aberdeen might rub off on Leeds and that Watson might bring along some of the young players. It did not work out. While there were matches Watson displayed his fitness and aggressive hard-running style, in others, he appeared bemused by the pace at which things happened around him. Chances he created by strong forward runs were too often let down by a poor final pass. Occasionally, too, Watson would be over-ambitious on the ball for a player with a poor first touch.

The emergence of Gray's young midfield stars Sellars and Sheridan emphasised Watson's lack of class and in December 1984 he returned to Scotland resuming his career in a league where clearly he felt more at home.

BORN: Aberdeen, 3.9.59.
GAMES: 42 (1). GOALS: 7.
OTHER CLUBS: Aberdeen 77/8-82/3 (96, 11);
Hearts 84/5-86/7 (56, 6);
Hibernian 87/8-88/9 (31, 3).

1983/84 - 1984/85

GEORGE McCLUSKEY

Some football fans have vivid memories of George McCluskey's brilliance. Alas for Leeds, they are Celtic supporters. When, for £160,000, the amiable Scot came to Elland Road from Parkhead where he had won two championship medals, his heart remained in Glasgow and he sometimes played with a certain absent-mindedness.

Yet in some ways McCluskey rather endeared himself to the Leeds supporters. It was clear he had considerable skill and an excellent first touch. On days when the midfield was motoring and balls arriving at his feet, McCluskey played the stylish striker and scored some sweet goals.

He was not, however, one for chasing the ball in the hope a seemingly lost cause might turn into a scoring chance. McCluskey had little appetite for pursuing balls knocked more in hope than in expectation over his head and into central channels. His appearances were fairly frequent in his first two seasons but by 1985/6, inconsistency saw him drift out of the side and few were surprised when he left Leeds to join Hibernian.

BORN: Hamilton, Scotland, 19.9.57.
GAMES: 66 (9). GOALS: 17.
OTHER CLUBS: Glasgow Celtic 75/6-82/3 (130, 54);
Hibernian 86/7-88/9 (86, 16);
Hamilton Academical 89/90-(94, 34).

1983/84 - 1985/86

RONNIE ROBINSON 1985/86-1986/87

Left-back. BORN: Sunderland, 22.12.66. GAMES: 27. GOALS: 0.
OTHER CLUBS: Doncaster Rovers 86/7-88/9 (113, 15);
West Bromwich Albion 88/89 (1, 0); Rotherham United 89/90 -
91/2 (86, 1); Peterborough United 91/2- (26, 0).

RONNIE ROBINSON

NEIL McNAB

NEIL McNAB 1982/83

Midfield. BORN: Greenock, 4.6.57. GAMES: 6. GOALS: 0.
OTHER CLUBS: Morton 72/3-73/4 (14, 0);
Tottenham Hotspur 73/4-78/9 (72, 3); Bolton Wanderers (78/9-
79/80 (35, 4); Brighton & Hove Albion 79/80-82/3 (103, 4);
Manchester City 83/4-89/90 (221, 16); Tranmere Rovers 90/1-
(51, 3) Huddersfield Town *(on loan)* 91/2 (10, 0).

BRIAN CASWELL 1985/86-1986/87

Left-back. BORN: Wednesbury, West Midlands, 14.2.56.
GAMES: 9. GOALS: 0.
OTHER CLUBS: Walsall 72/3-84/5 (402, 17);
Doncaster Rovers 85/86 (15, 2);
Wolverhampton Wanderers *(on loan)* 86/7 (1, 0).

BRIAN CASWELL

JOHN McGREGOR

JOHN McGREGOR 1985/86

Midfield/defender. BORN: Airdrie, 5.1.63. GAMES: 5. GOALS: 0.
OTHER CLUBS: Queen's Park 79/80 (105, 19); Liverpool (0, 0);
St Mirren *(on loan)* 83/84 (5, 1); Glasgow Rangers 87/8 (25, 0).

LYNDON SIMMONDS 1984/85-1985/86

Forward. BORN: Pontypool, Gwent, 11.11.86.
GAMES: 6 (3). GOALS: 3. OTHER CLUBS: Swansea City *(on loan)*
86/7 (8, 1); Rochdale 86/7-87/8 (65, 22).

TREVOR SWINBURNE

LYNDON SYMMONDS

TREVOR SWINBURNE 1985/86

Goalkeeper. BORN: East Rainton, Co. Durham, 20.6.53.
GAMES: 2. GOALS: 0.
OTHER CLUBS: Sunderland 70/1-76/7 (10, 0); Carlisle United
77/8-82/3 (248, 0) Brentford 83/4-84/5 (45, 0); Doncaster Rovers
(on loan) 85/6 (4, 0); Lincoln City 85/6-86/7 (34, 0).

JOHN BUCKLEY 1986/87-1987/88

Winger. BORN: East Kilbride, Lanarkshire 10.5.62.
GAMES: 6 (5). GOALS: 1.
OTHER CLUBS: Partick Thistle 82/3-83/4 (45, 5); Doncaster
Rovers 84/5-85/6, 87/8 *(on loan)* (90, 11); Leicester City *(on loan)*
86/7 (5, 0); Rotherham United 87/8-90/1 (105, 13);

JOHN BUCKLEY

SIMON GRAYSON

PETER MAGUIRE

DAVID HARLE

NIGEL THOMPSON

SIMON GRAYSON 1987/88

Midfield. BORN: Ripon, North Yorkshire, 16.12.69.
GAMES: 2. GOALS: 0.
OTHER CLUBS: Leicester City 91/2 (11, 0).

PETER MUMBY 1987/88-1988/89

Forward. BORN: Bradford, 22.2.69. GAMES: 3 (5). GOALS: 1.
OTHER CLUBS: Shamrock Rovers, Ireland *(on loan)* 88/9;
Burnley 89/90-90/1 (45, 9).

PETER MAGUIRE 1987/88

Forward. BORN: Holmfirth, West Yorkshire, 11.9.69.
GAMES: 2. GOALS: 0.
OTHER CLUBS: Huddersfield Town 89/90-90/1 (7, 0);
Stockport County *(on loan)* 90/1 (2, 0).

KEVIN NOTEMAN 1987-88

Forward. BORN: Preston, 15.10.69. GAMES: 0 (1). GOALS: 0.
OTHER CLUBS: Doncaster Rovers 89/90-91/2 (107, 20);
Mansfield Town 91/2- (6, 0).

DAVID HARLE 1985/86

Midfield. BORN: Denaby, near Doncaster, 15.8.63.
GAMES: 3. GOALS: 0.
OTHER CLUBS: Doncaster Rovers 79/80-81/82, 83/4-85/6,
90/1- (187, 23); Exeter City 82/3-83/4 (43, 6);
Bristol City 85/6-86/7 (23, 2); Scunthorpe United 86/7-88/9
(87,10); Peterborough United 88/9-89/90 (22, 2).

RONNIE SINCLAIR 1986/87

Goalkeeper. BORN: Stirling, 19.10.64. GAMES: 9. GOALS: 0.
OTHER CLUBS: Wrexham *(on loan from Nottingham Forest)* 83/4
(11, 0); Halifax Town *(on loan)* 86/7, 88/9 (14, 0);
Bristol City 89/90-90/1 (44, 0); Walsall *(on loan)* 91/2 (11, 0);
Stoke City 91/2- (24, 0).

NIGEL THOMPSON 1983/84-1986/87

Defender/midfield. BORN: Leeds, 1.3.67.
GAMES: 8 (1). GOALS: 0.
OTHER CLUBS: Rochdale *(on loan)* 87/8 (5, 0);
Chesterfield 87/8-89/90 (20, 1).

PETER MUMBY

KEVIN NOTEMAN

RONNIE SINCLAIR

SCOTT SELLARS

That Scott Sellars should survive and flourish in league football is in triumphant defiance of pessimists who believe frail-looking players with delicate skills stand no chance of making the grade. For when Sellars made his debut as a 17-year-old against Shrewsbury in May 1983, he appeared so youthful and mild, one could only fear what might befall him when the going got tough.

But a good football brain, artistry, and willingness have kept Scott Sellars going. From his junior days, he was ambitious to strike the long, constructive pass even if his strength were not up to it. Pitched into the Leeds team on the left side of midfield alongside John Sheridan, his senior by nearly 14 months, Sellars grew up quickly, learning to take the ball under pressure then fashion openings from which to play accurate passes.

During afternoons, Eddie Gray would take his two midfield protégés to one side to polish up their ball control. Few footballers struck a sweeter ball with the left foot than did Sellars, a player whose skills and stature recalled Terry Hibbitt. All who saw it will remember Sellars' pearl of a goal against Wimbledon during the 5-2 home win of December 1984, a chip from the left edge of the penalty area that curled into the top of the net.

That year, there was the mirage of promotion but the team was not quite strong enough; and for Sellars and Leeds, 1985/6 was difficult when a poor start saw Gray sacked and Billy Bremner appointed successor. After requesting a transfer following Bremner's tactical reorganisation of the side, Sellars was sold to Blackburn Rovers for a song - £20,000 - where he has continued to grace the game. And although he now knows all the league has to throw at him, some feel the best of Sellars has yet to be seen.

BORN: Sheffield 27.11.65.
GAMES: 80 (4). GOALS: 13.
OTHER CLUBS: Blackburn Rovers 86/7- (199, 35).

1982/83 - 1985/86

ANDY RITCHIE

Many Leeds fans recall vividly their first dose of Andy Ritchie. It was as a teenage star in March 1979, wearing the red of Manchester United, that he savaged the Leeds defence and scored a hat-trick. Leeds crashed 4-1 and such a humiliation at the hands of the old enemy, wrought by a precocious teenager, was too painful to be forgotten quickly.

Ritchie's admirers continue to be surprised he has not achieved more following his virtuoso arrival on the first division stage. That is not to belittle his career at Manchester United, Brighton, Leeds and Oldham; yet at times, he has displayed his talents so profusely, almost as if self-consciously demonstrating a text-book repertoire of the striker's arts, that surely he has been worth considering as England material.

Yet with the exception of his first club, Andy Ritchie has spent his career in unfashionable surroundings. Leeds, in the second division, were well away from the limelight save for their hooligan followers. Ritchie has been prone to bouts of inconsistency but the memories of his days at Leeds are mostly good. Apart from his portfolio of goals struck with crisp precision from his boot, or headed with assured accuracy, the Leeds management knew Ritchie had the bravery and technique to play the role of target man; that when long balls were played up to him, they would stick until support arrived.

If Ritchie's pace was not his greatest asset, his first touch was so clever and his football brain so acute he could make time for himself and others. Almost everything he did had some style. If Ritchie lacked anything, perhaps it was hunger and drive; at Leeds he was a good natured player who rarely got upset and perhaps tolerated losing too easily. The team around him lacked fire in its belly. A transfer to Oldham for £50,000 in August 1987, and promotion to the first division, where he belongs, have brought Ritchie more exposure, and television audiences have seen some awesome performances from him. Too little, too late, for England, but beautiful to behold.

BORN: Manchester, 28.11.60.
GAMES: 149 (10). GOALS: 44.
OTHER CLUBS: Manchester United 77/8-80/1 (33, 13);
Brighton 80/1-82/3 (89, 23);
Oldham Athletic 87/8 - (149, 66).

1982/83 - 1986/87

IAN BAIRD

On a bitter day in January 1987, Leeds United were making laboured efforts to knock Telford United out of the FA Cup. Drawing 1-1, no better than their non-league opponents on a frozen pitch, five minutes remained when Ian Baird gathered the ball on the right, brushed aside his challengers and beat the goalkeeper with a low shot from an acute angle. With that stylish winning goal, the only moment of class in a wretched game, Leeds began a cup run that led to the semi-finals and the nearest the team came to glory in the 1980s.

Ian Baird had been signed from Southampton for £50,000 in 1985 and the inconsistency of his career thereafter never seemed to do his talents full justice. For Yorkshire-born Baird had the attributes of a quality striker: strength, aerial power, the ability to hold up the ball and neat ball control, with enough skill to turn and outwit defenders.

Baird's playing character could show bravery one moment, rashness the next. Even making allowances for the rigorous nature of his trade, he allowed himself to be sucked into too many acrimonious situations. At times he seemed to pick up as many bookings for futile retaliatory fouls and dissent as goals, and wasted many weeks serving suspensions.

Yet Baird's aggressive spirit was appreciated by the Elland Road crowd. He was never anxious to leave the club, where he hoped he had a future, yet was transferred first to Portsmouth by Billy Bremner (who bought him back a year later) and then to Middlesbrough by Howard Wilkinson after the arrival of Lee Chapman. Baird's talents were rarely tested in the first division. A combination of ill-luck and difficult temperament may have conspired to deny him success at the level his abilities merit. Yet he served Leeds well and provided some fine goals which allowed his fans to dream of better days.

BORN: Rotherham 1.4.64. GAMES: 182 (2). GOALS: 57.
HONOURS: Second Division Championship 89/90.
OTHER CLUBS: Southampton 82/3-84/5 (22, 5); Cardiff City *(on loan)* 83/4 (12, 6); Newcastle United *(on loan)* 84/5 (5, 1); Portsmouth 87/8 (20, 1); Middlesbrough 89/90-90/1 (63, 19); Hearts 91/2 - (28, 5).

1984/85 - 1986/87 & 1987/88 - 1989/90

MERVYN DAY

By the time Mervyn Day arrived at Leeds, he had lived down his image as the dazzling young sportsman who had failed to fulfil his talents. Apart from football, he played hockey and cricket for Essex schoolboys and his spectacular early appearances in goal for West Ham brought talk of an England career. But after four seasons as first choice at Upton Park, in which he won an FA Cup winners medal in 1975, Day was to battle with injury, loss of form and confidence, and was eventually ousted by Phil Parkes. He then spent four years of relative obscurity with Orient.

Eddie Gray signed Day from Aston Villa in February 1985 as replacement for David Harvey. The idea was to provide valuable experience behind a young defence still learning its trade. Day was one of the few constant figures in the Leeds side over the next five years, first choice under Billy Bremner and Howard Wilkinson until Leeds returned to division one. For £30,000, he was a bargain.

With the extremes of his playing past behind him, Day settled in well at Elland Road: a dependable figure who commanded his area well, still agile and brave, and only occasionally prone to errors of judgement. In his early thirties - when many goalkeepers achieve their peak - he was commonly considered the best outside the first division. Day served Leeds nobly in 1986/7, when the club so nearly won promotion and an FA Cup final place, and in the championship season of 1989/90.

BORN: Chelmsford, Essex, 26.6.55. GAMES: 249. GOALS: 0.
HONOURS: Second Division Championship 89/90.
OTHER CLUBS: West Ham United 73/4-78/9 (194, 0);
Orient 79/80-82/3 (168, 0);
Aston Villa 83/4-84/5 (30, 0);
Luton Town *(on loan)* 91/2 (4, 0).

1984/85 - 1990/91

MARK GAVIN

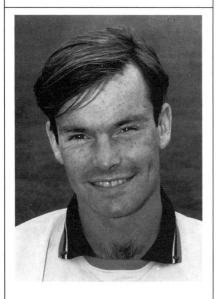

Mark Gavin was re-signed by Eddie Gray having been given a free transfer by Allan Clarke in 1982. Gray saw potential in the young Scottish left-winger and appreciated Gavin's willingness to receive the ball and his knack of firing accurate crosses into the penalty area.

Certainly there were games when Mark Gavin's neat, tricky wing play was an attractive feature of the Leeds attack. Gavin was among the fittest players at Elland Road and probably at his best with his manager on the field behind him. One of Gray's great managerial gifts lay in directing and supporting his young talent.

Unlike some of Gray's other protégés, Gavin failed to achieve enough consistency for his career at Elland Road to take off. During 1984/5, Frank Gray took over the number 11 shirt and in July 1985 Gavin was transferred to Carlisle United, the first of several subsequent clubs.

BORN: Baillieston, Glasgow, 10.10.63.
GAMES: 24 (11). GOALS: 4.
OTHER CLUBS:
Hartlepool United (on loan) 84/5 (7, 0);
Carlisle United 85/6 (13, 1);
Bolton Wanderers 85/6-87/8 (49, 3);
Rochdale 87/8 (23, 6);
Heart of Midlothian 87/8-88/9 (9, 0);
Bristol City 88/9-90/1, 91/2- (83, 6);
Watford 90/1 (13, 0).

1982/83 - 1984/85

PETER SWAN

While Peter Swan never had a position in the Leeds team of his own, he proved a useful squad man, capable of playing in defence and as an auxiliary striker. Although no great stylist - he began as a centre-forward but because he lacked technique was converted to a centre back by the Leeds coaching staff - Swan had a vigorous bustling style.

Swan was signed as an apprentice by Eddie Gray but made his debut in a Full Members' Cup match against Manchester City on October 14 1985, three days after Gray was sacked and Leeds were managerless. In 1987/8, as Billy Bremner, Gray's successor, cast around to find his best side (and in doing so used 28 players), Swan had something approaching a good run in the first team, scoring eight times during 25 league outings in various positions.

Swan played just one game the following season - against Hull - but clearly had made an impression on the management. For it was to Boothferry Park that Swan was transferred as Leeds' new manager Howard Wilkinson concluded one of several shrewd business deals, realising £200,000 when selling him to the Tigers in March 1989.

BORN: Leeds 28.9.66.
GAMES: 49 (6). GOALS: 13.
OTHER CLUBS: Hull City 88/9-90/1 (80, 24); Port Vale 91/2- (28, 3).

1985/86 - 1988/89

TERRY PHELAN

Terry Phelan was another young player whose potential was assessed shrewdly by Eddie Gray but who blossomed elsewhere. That he did not have an extended run at Elland Road may be down to his being a victim of managerial experiments.

When brought in by Gray against Shrewsbury in September 1985, Phelan made an eye-catching debut at left-back; among the best the Leeds management had seen from a newcomer. Above all, he showed pace and stamina, and a great appetite for work. But when Gray was sacked and Billy Bremner came to Leeds, Phelan had played just a handful of games. Still only 18, Phelan's career had not developed sufficient momentum to persuade his new boss that he, rather than a more experienced professional, was the natural choice for the number 3 shirt.

At the end of 1985/6, Terry Phelan was allowed to slip away on a free transfer. He made an immediate impact at Swansea and within a year was enjoying first division football at Wimbledon; within two, had an FA Cup Winners medal. Another fine prospect had had the misfortune to be at Elland Road at the wrong time.

BORN: Manchester, 16.3.67.
GAMES: 15 (2). GOALS: 0
HONOURS:
8 Republic of Ireland Caps 91.
OTHER CLUBS:
Swansea City 86/7 (45, 0);
Wimbledon 87/8- (158, 2).

1985/86

IAN SNODIN

For most football careerists, spending five years at Doncaster Rovers might not seem the ideal way to get on. Yet from that modest shop window, Ian Snodin was awarded first England youth then England Under 21 caps. His skill, aggression and maturity in midfield attracted the attention of many big clubs but it was to Leeds, showing signs of stirring under Eddie Gray, that Snodin went for £200,000.

The lesson of 1984/5, when lack of bite had seen Leeds surrender too many points to secure promotion, had not been lost on Gray. A midfield stiffened by the inclusion of Snodin might allow the team to make further progress. And while he went into a side that made a shaky start, Snodin's qualities were obvious. He was an excellent tackler, providing the aggressive ball winning skills Leeds had lacked, had remarkable pace, and had the good first touch that denotes a player of high quality.

Gray made Snodin team captain as a replacement for Peter Lorimer. With his vision and position in the centre of things he was ideal for the job. But despite his footballing maturity, with Snodin's aggression came flashes of temper that could land him in needless trouble. And in some his early games, he disappointed the Leeds management by a tendency to fade out of games after showing his calibre for twenty minutes or so.

Billy Bremner, his manager at Doncaster, inherited Snodin along with the Leeds job and stuck with him. Snodin's displays were monitored by first division clubs and it was with great reluctance that Bremner, who had hopes of building a team around him, felt forced to sell Snodin to Everton for £840,000 in January 1987. Snodin's first season at Goodison was his most glorious, for he won a League Championship medal but since, what should have been a fine career has been blighted by serious injury.

BORN: Thrybergh, Rotherham 15.8.63.
GAMES: 55. GOALS: 8.
OTHER CLUBS: Doncaster Rovers 79/80-84/5 (188, 25);
Everton 86/7 - (71, 2).

1985/86 - 1986/87

JOHN SHERIDAN

John Sheridan stayed a long time at Leeds hoping to achieve first division football. He was, by general agreement, the finest midfielder in the lower leagues, and on his day among the best anywhere, maturing so rapidly after his introduction to the team as an 18-year-old in November 1982 it seems incredible his talents had been discarded by Manchester City.

Eddie Gray was trying to construct a team that might play its way out of the second division with wit and skill rather than by brute force. John Sheridan, playing on the right, rapidly became the focal point of constructive play, shouldering the midfield burden with the younger and slighter Scott Sellars. If a lack of steel stood between Leeds and promotion to the first division in the mid 1980s, Sheridan quickly learned to look after himself, sometimes with a rashness that landed him in trouble.

John Sheridan had a terrific repertoire of skills. His long accurate passes were delicious to watch and he showed a clear understanding of everything going on that led him to play the most intelligent ball available. His shots were exhilarating, whether volleyed or struck with spectacular power and accuracy from free kicks. From one such, a brilliant wily chip against Charlton Athletic in the play-offs final replay of 1986/7, he put first division football within Leeds' grasp before the dogged Londoners snatched it away with two goals in the dying minutes of extra time.

From the outset, Sheridan played with remarkable composure for one so young. He made a swift and complete recovery from a broken leg sustained at Barnsley in October 1983 and the experience never inhibited him from taking responsibilities in hard-fought midfield battles. Leeds could have asked no more of him than he gave. It was one of the more eccentric episodes in Brian Clough's history to pay £650,000 for Sheridan in August 1989 then have him languish for four months, giving him just one outing in a League Cup game against Huddersfield. When rescued by Sheffield Wednesday, Sheridan thrived once more, showing his relish for the big time with a thunderous goal that defeated Manchester United in the 1991 Rumbelows League Cup Final and brought the trophy to Hillsborough for the first time.

BORN: Manchester 1.10.64.
GAMES: 255 (6). GOALS: 52.
HONOURS: 13 Republic of Ireland Caps 88-91.
OTHER CLUBS: Nottingham Forest 89/90 (0, 0);
Sheffield Wednesday 89/90 - (97, 17).

1982/83 - 1988/89

MARK AIZLEWOOD

It was a pity Mark Aizlewood's career at Leeds ended in disrepute. Although not the most gifted defensive midfielder, he would never flinch from a battle; and battles were the order of the day for a team trying to scramble out of the second division. Aizlewood had experienced two successful campaigns with Charlton and Luton, and only missed out at the death with Leeds after joining the club in February 1987.

Aizlewood was a durable, hard-tackling journeyman, at his best winning the ball and helping avert danger. His presence allowed John Sheridan to play further forward and shed some responsibilities for foraging for the ball. Aizlewood's positional sense at the back was generally sound but his passing inconsistent: good one day, wasteful the next.

He was made captain by Billy Bremner and had the forceful personality to gee up those around him. But Aizlewood also had a pugnacious side that led him into silly confrontations. When, near the end of the 1988/9 season, he was going through a bad spell and incurring the displeasure of the Leeds crowd, he reacted with a rude gesture to barracking supporters after scoring against Walsall and was immediately substituted.

Aizlewood's new manager Howard Wilkinson, who demanded high standards of behaviour as well as performance, stripped him of the captaincy and suspended him for two weeks. In the summer, the disaffected Aizlewood transferred to Bradford City for £200,000. Not for the first or the last time, his career, which contained a number of highlights and commendable performances, was marred by a display of immature rashness.

BORN: Newport, South Wales, 1.10.59. GAMES: 74 (5). GOALS: 3.
HONOURS: 33 Wales Caps 86–92.
OTHER CLUBS: Newport County 75/6–77/8 (38, 1);
Luton Town 77/8–82/3 (98, 3);
Charlton Athletic 82/3–86/7 (160, 9); Bradford City 89–90 (39, 1);
Bristol City 90/1 - (75, 2).

1986/87 - 1988/89

BRENDAN ORMSBY

The damaged cartilage sustained by Brendan Ormsby as Leeds strained every nerve and muscle to gain promotion in 1987 effectively ended his career at Elland Road. It happened during the final play-off of the season against Charlton Athletic; a melo-dramatic finale to an epic campaign in which Ormsby's efforts as team captain and fearless defender had been central.

Ormsby, who was signed in March 1986 and cost just £65,000, was undoubtedly one of Billy Bremner's best buys. He played with a great sense of urgency and, alongside the unfussily efficient Jack Ashurst, helped bring order to the centre of the Leeds defence. One of his principal assets was bravery, a willingness to plunge into dangerous areas where hard knocks were likely and the rewards uncertain.

Occasionally Ormsby's judgement betrayed him; never more publicly than when he failed to clear his lines in the FA Cup semi-final against Coventry and allowed the Sky Blues to fashion an equalising goal. But his thrusting presence more than compensated for any shortcomings, in defence as well as in attack, where his late headed winner against Queen's Park Rangers in the FA Cup fifth round, although unsophisticated, is one from the 1980s many Leeds fans might choose to take to their desert island.

BORN: Birmingham 1.10.60. GAMES: 56. GOALS: 7.
OTHER CLUBS: Aston Villa 78/9-85/6 (117, 4);
Shrewsbury Town *(on loan)* 89/90 (1, 0);
Doncaster Rovers 90/91- (77, 8).

1985/86 - 1988/89

TOMMY WRIGHT

Tommy Wright's piercing runs into the heart of enemy territory and assurance in front of goal were thrilling to watch. He made his debut for Leeds in 1983 as a 17-year-old, scoring against Fulham in a 1-1 draw, and making a similar startling impression on the game as had Terry Connor six years earlier.

Wright's game was based on his speed and quickness of reaction. He could throw close markers by turning rapidly, or chase long balls played through the middle. He had good close control - a legacy of his more youthful days as an outside-left - and was steady in front of goal, showing great composure when left one on one with the goalkeeper.

His career at Leeds was interrupted by injury and under Billy Bremner, he found difficulty in regaining his place. Wright was sold to Oldham for £80,000 in October 1986 where his speed and scoring instincts continued to bedevil defences; and then to Leicester in August 1989.

BORN: Dunfermline 10.1.66.
GAMES: 80 (11). GOALS: 28.
OTHER CLUBS: Oldham Athletic 86/7-88/9 (112, 23);
Leicester City 89/90- (126, 21).

1982/83 - 1985/86

NEIL ASPIN

Few players gave Leeds more over the seasons than Neil Aspin. His talents may have been modest compared with some past Leeds defenders but Aspin never let the side down for want of trying. He was pitched into the side as a 16-year-old by Allan Clarke in Leeds' relegation season but it was during the club's second division days Aspin eventually became a regular at right-back.

Aspin's pure footballing ability was quite limited. He is not remembered for his stylish passing or exciting overlapping play. But he was an honest professional who would get stuck into the job, and became more confident and assured with maturity. Covering and tackling were his principal assets rather than dwelling on the ball thereafter. At six feet tall, Aspin was a fairly commanding figure in the air who could contribute to aerial attacks.

His commitment to whatever cause was going at Elland Road was unquestionable. As much as for anything he did on the field, Aspin is celebrated at Elland Road for postponing his wedding so he could play in Leeds' FA Cup semi-final against Coventry in 1987. Aspin had more than 200 league games behind him yet was still only 24 when Howard Wilkinson transferred him to Port Vale in July 1989 and replaced him with Mel Sterland.

BORN: Gateshead 12.4.65.
GAMES: 233 (3). GOALS: 6.
OTHER CLUBS: Port Vale 89/90- (122, 1).

1981/82- 1988/89

BOB TAYLOR

Some who have watched Bob Taylor are surprised that, after six years in the game, his apparent potential has not been fulfilled more consistently. From his debut against Millwall in April 1986 - a match Leeds needed to win to stave off lingering fears of relegation - the lean and mobile young striker made a good impression, displaying an intuitive sense for the half-chance.

Taylor became a regular in 1987, arriving from Northern League side Horden Colliery Welfare and played, at various times, alongside Bobby Davison and then Ian Baird. He was not in the battering-ram mould of striker but more reliant on a good first touch, well-timed jumps and sharp reflexes for his scoring opportunities. On a good day, he was hard for any defence to contain but there were other matches when he was anonymous and he appeared reluctant to try to make things happen in the midst of a mean defence.

Taylor left for Bristol City in March 1989 in an exchange deal that brought Carl Shutt to Elland Road. The following season, Taylor made hay among third division defences and was top scorer in City's promotion season but thereafter lost form, became unsettled, and was transferred to West Bromwich Albion in 1991/2.

BORN: Easington, Co. Durham, 3.2.67.
GAMES: 39 (10). GOALS: 12.
OTHER CLUBS: Bristol City 89/90-91/2 (106, 49);
West Bromwich Albion 91/2- (17, 6).

1985/86 - 1988/89

JOHN PEARSON

Sometimes Leeds fans would gaze at the ungainly John Pearson and wonder quite what he was for. Here was a striker who rarely scored, who lacked pace, who had the turning circle of an oil-tanker, yet still got into the side. How?

His real asset, in the eyes of Leeds managers, was as a distraction whose presence in the side created chances for others. At six feet two, the amiable Pearson was likely to win many high balls, as indeed he did, sometimes simply by standing on tip toe, so it seemed, rather than leaping into the air. As long as Pearson was about, defences could not quite afford to relax.

Pearson was used as a substitute almost as often as he started a game but could often provide late afternoon disquiet for opposing defenders. He was bought by Billy Bremner from Charlton in January 1987 for £70,000 and had his most productive spell for Leeds towards the end of that season. Pearson survived Howard Wilkinson's wholesale reconstruction of the Leeds side, continuing to make occasional appearances that were sometimes useful if never ornamental.

BORN: Sheffield 1.9.63.
GAMES: 65 (56). GOALS: 12.
OTHER CLUBS: Sheffield Wednesday 80/1-84/5 (115, 24);
Charlton Athletic 85/6-86/7 (61, 15);
Barnsley 91/2 (10, 1);
Hull City *(on loan)* 91/2 (15, 0).

1986/87 - 1990/91

KEITH EDWARDS

The arrival at Leeds of Keith Edwards sent a current of excitement running through Elland Road. Wherever he played, he had never failed to score. But at Leeds, he would be remembered for contributions that brought theatrical climaxes to crucial matches. When he first arrived, his scoring touch deserted him though several times he was denied by the crossbar or post.

No Leeds fan will forget, as the tie seemed to have slipped from their team, Keith Edwards' headed equaliser that put the FA Cup semi-final against Coventry into extra time, A month later, during a game of crazy turbulence at Oldham during the play-offs, it was an Edwards goal that sunk the home side almost on full-time, a stunning immediate reply to what had looked like the Latics' winning goal.

Edwards was a player with a delicate touch who liked to feed off a big target man. He was less keen on scrapping for possession and once told the Leeds management he preferred playing football with the Elland Road youngsters. Yet his sixth sense for the half chance and coolness in front of goal brought some rich dramatic moments to Elland Road.

BORN: Stockton-on-Tees 16.7.57.
GAMES 33 (17). GOALS: 9.
OTHER CLUBS: Sheffield United 75/6-77/8, 81/2-85/6
(261, 143); Hull City 78/9-81/2, 87/8-89/90 (187, 86);
Aberdeen 87/8 (9, 2); Stockport County 89/90 (27, 10);
Huddersfield Town 89/90-90/1 (28, 8);
Plymouth Argyle *(on loan)* 90/1 (3, 1).

1986/87 - 1987/88

JACK ASHURST

The signing of Jack Ashurst, a centre-half in his early thirties who after a spell with Sunderland made an unflamboyant career with Blackpool and Carlisle, suggested penury rather than ambition was the driving force at Elland Road. His arrival at Leeds was hardly to be trumpeted from the rooftops. Yet, at £35,000, Ashurst was among Billy Bremner's shrewdest investments and provided a steadiness in the central defence worthy of someone costing ten times as much.

For two seasons, the Scots-born Ashurst was remarkably consistent. He missed only four league games, and appeared in all the cup and play-off matches that brought Leeds' 1986/7 season to its boiling climax. Ashurst, however, with scant first division experience, was a model of coolness, good in the air, and covered the ground quickly for a man of his age. When Ashurst played alongside Brendan Ormsby, the defence had a solid, assured air about it; Ormsby's vigorous game being complemented by Ashurst's vision and tidiness.

Ashurst, who was made captain in Snodin's and Aizlewood's absence, was a classic late developer. Had he, or others realised his potential earlier, a career as a first division defender probably would not have been beyond him.

BORN: Coatbridge, Lanarkshire, 12.10.54.
GAMES: 105 (1). GOALS: 1.
OTHER CLUBS: Sunderland 72/3-79/80 (140, 4);
Blackpool 79/80-80/81 (53, 3); Carlisle United 81/2-85/6
(194, 2); Doncaster Rovers 88/9- (111, 1).

1986/87-1988/89

BOBBY McDONALD

Bobby McDonald was another defender who had done the rounds before coming, inexpensively, to Leeds in 1987. But he played with the assurance of someone acquainted with top class football and had just left behind an Oxford United team which had enjoyed the most successful phase in its history.

At almost 32, McDonald was a seasoned and mature left-back but by no means past it. Experience at the top level with Coventry and Manchester City taught him to read the game well and develop an excellent positional sense. He still had a good turn of speed and the skill and presence of mind to fashion attacking moves from the back, able to strike excellent long balls with his left foot.

Bobby McDonald slotted comfortably into the team that was pushing for the first division. While he would not have expected a long career at Elland Road, McDonald must have hoped for more than just half a season; for injury restricted him to just two appearances in 1987/8. At the end of the season he was granted a free transfer and joined non-league VS Rugby.

BORN: Aberdeen, 13.4.55.
GAMES: 24. GOALS: 1.
OTHER CLUBS: Aston Villa 72/3-76/7 (39, 3);
Coventry City 76/7-80/81 (160, 14);
Manchester City 80/1-83/4 (96, 11);
Oxford United 83/4-86/7 (94, 14).

1986/87 - 1987/88

BOBBY DAVISON

It is sometimes Bobby Davison's misfortune to be damned with faint praise as a hustling, hard-running centre-forward. Those who have watched him closely know better: for while he is not flashy, he has talents that are underestimated.

Davison's performances helped lay the foundations of Leeds' Second Division Championship season, even though injury prevented him from taking part in many of the final laps. Some of his goals derived from the strong direct running and ability to keep a cool head - even if forced to shoot from an acute angle - that are Davison hallmarks; others, such as that which sunk Bradford City at Valley Parade in October 1989, came from superbly-timed jumps and deserve inclusion in any coaching video designed to illustrate the art of heading.

At Derby, and in two previous seasons at Leeds, the Bobby Davison strike-rate rarely failed. He was also adept at shielding the ball while waiting for support and creating such panic and disorder when bursting into enemy territory that defenders were forced into reckless and costly challenges. And if scoring chances were not arriving on a silver salver, Davison would forage in midfield where he had the clout to win possession then create chances either for himself or team-mates.

Bobby Davison is appreciated at Leeds for the vigour and relish with which he played his football. His skills were never brazen but it takes talent to score as many quality goals as has Davison over the years.

BORN: South Shields 17.7.59. GAMES: 85 (15). GOALS: 33.
OTHER CLUBS: Huddersfield Town 80/1 (2, 0);
Halifax Town 81/2-82/3 (63, 29);
Derby County 82/3-87/8, (on loan) 91/2 (203, 91);
Sheffield United (on loan) 91/2 (9, 4).

1987/88-

MICKY ADAMS

Leeds manager Billy Bremner had spent a season mending and making do at left back before signing Micky Adams from Coventry City in January 1987. His arrival coincided with a surge in the team's fortunes and the end of aberrant performances that had included, one month earlier, a 7-2 drubbing at Stoke City.

Speed and energy were the hallmarks of Adams' game. He had played in midfield but at Leeds his role was mostly that of a busy, compact defender. He was quick to the tackle even if not born to the role of dominant stopper despite his natural aggression. Such was not his preferred style anyway, for Adams liked to start attacking moves from the back even though, on some of his less distinguished days, he gave the ball away through ill-directed passing.

But when playing well, Adams showed the pace and quick reactions to turn defence into attack, and, with darting runs and crosses from the left flank could cause panic in the opposition penalty area. In defence he read the game well and could avert danger early by making a timely interception. Although excluded from Howard Wilkinson's plans for a grand future at Leeds, Adams, sold to Southampton in March 1989 for £250,000, became a first-team regular at The Dell, and showed he had the character and ability to ply his trade at the top level.

BORN: Sheffield, 8.11.61.
GAMES: 87 (1). GOALS: 3. OTHER CLUBS: Gillingham 79/70-82/3 (92, 5); Coventry City 83/4-86/7 (90, 9); Southampton 88/9- (86, 3).

1986/87 - 1988/89

DAVID RENNIE

David Rennie may have no more glorious day than the Sunday afternoon he headed home a corner into the Coventry net and fuelled dreams of a Wembley appearance for tens of thousands of Leeds fans.
His goal, in that FA Cup semi-final of 1987, was the pinnacle of one of the team's most enthralling performances for a decade. Several Leeds men played above themselves including Rennie, a left-sided defensive midfield player with perhaps not quite the talent to be described as versatile.

Before joining Leeds in January 1986 for £50,000, Rennie, a Scotsman who won youth caps for his country, spent four years at Leicester City, much of it in the reserves. But he went straight into the Leeds first team, and was probably at his best playing centre-back where he put his ability in the air to good use.

Rennie was a workmanlike player but lacked the speed, mobility and vision to be an effective midfielder. Although short of the quality and speed of reaction for the first division - despite Billy Bremner's aspirations for the club - Rennie rarely gave less than his best and brought Leeds a handsome profit when sold by Howard Wilkinson to Bristol City for £200,000 in August 1989.

BORN: Edinburgh, 29.8.64.
GAMES: 109 (6). GOALS: 6.
OTHER CLUBS:
Leicester City 82/3-85/6 (21, 1);
Bristol City 89/90-91/2 (104, 8);
Birmingham City 91/2 (16, 1).

1985/86 - 1988/89

JOHN STILES

If a footballer's future could be determined by enthusiasm alone, John Stiles, son of the redoubtable Manchester United and England wing-half Nobby, would have been a candidate for the top. But if he had inherited that quality from his father, he lacked the concentrated aggression and speed of thought that sustained Nobby's career.

For the lesser of two players from different generations such comparisons are invidious, if inevitable. Yet in 1986/7, as Leeds threatened a remarkable double of escaping the second division and reaching Wembley, John made a tenacious contribution in midfield where he chased and harried and, when given the time, could deliver a sweet pass.

His game though was based largely on honest toil. It took him a second too long to translate his more creative impulses into action; the crucial second that divides the great and the good midfielders from the journeymen. Yet John Stiles might at least have enjoyed longer at second division level had not his ambitions been thwarted by injuries over the next two seasons. He was eventually sold to Doncaster Rovers for £40,000 in August 1989.

BORN: Manchester, 6.5.64.
GAMES: 60 (17). GOALS: 3.
OTHER CLUBS:
Shamrock Rovers, Ireland;
Vancouver Whitecaps, Canada;
Doncaster Rovers 89/90- (88, 2);
Rochdale (on loan) 91/2 (4, 0).

1984/85 - 1988/89

GARY WILLIAMS

With the acquisition of Gary Williams, Billy Bremner hoped to bring experience at the highest level - his new recruit had won a league championship and the European Cup with Aston Villa in the early 1980s - and some refinement to the Leeds defence. But he had also brought a player perhaps not wholly free from earlier injuries.

Certainly at second division level, Gary Williams' quality was apparent. He was a footballing defender rather than blood and thunder merchant, also capable of playing in midfield. During 1987/8, Williams was more or less a regular on the right side of the field, a neat, industrious player whose accurate passing or running out of defence could initiate attacks down the flanks. He would also overlap and provide crosses into the penalty area good enough to disturb the heart of many a defence.

There was little to suggest Williams' tidy performances might not continue the following season but injury and the accession of Howard Wilkinson knocked his career at Elland Road off its equilibrium. He made just three league appearances under Wilkinson's management before joining Watford on a free transfer in January 1990.

BORN: Wolverhampton, 17.6.60.
GAMES: 44 (1). GOALS: 3.
OTHER CLUBS: Aston Villa 78/9-86/7 (240, 0);
Walsall *(on loan)* 79/80 (9, 0); Watford 89/90-91/2 (42, 0);
Bradford City 91/2- (17, 0).

1987/88 - 1988/89

NOEL BLAKE

The prospect of Noel Blake playing in a Leeds United shirt was not, to many supporters, particularly appetising, for he had been a component of Alan Ball's uncouth and unappealing Portsmouth team of the mid 1980s. Moreover, he had arrived on a free transfer and was unlikely to inspire confidence among those who feel that if a player is given away he cannot be any good.

Undoubtedly Jamaican-born Blake was not pretty to watch and few of the finer footballing arts entered his repertoire. Yet he confounded many by doing a good steady job in the heart of the Leeds defence. His speciality was soaking up pressure, winning aerial duels, defending at all costs, if necessary with recourse to the mean streak that his off-field geniality belied.

Blake appeared to thrive under pressure. To keep him interested in a match he needed constantly to be employed. Creativity was not his strong suit - though he could strike the ball well with his right foot- but he knew his capabilities and stuck to them. Blake spent a worthy season and a half subduing opposition forwards until Howard Wilkinson transferred him to Stoke in January 1990 for £175,000; as tidy a piece of business as ever the Leeds manager did.

BORN: Kingston, Jamaica, 12.1.62. GAMES: 57 (1). GOALS: 4.
OTHER CLUBS: Aston Villa 79/80-81/2 (4, 0);
Shrewsbury Town *(on loan)* 81/2 (6, 0);
Birmingham City 82/3-83/4 (76, 5);
Portsmouth 84/5-87/8 (144, 10); Stoke City 89/90- (75, 3).

1988/89 - 1989/90

VINNIE JONES

The transfer of Vinnie Jones from Wimbledon to Leeds United in June 1989 was relished by soccer's more cynical on-lookers. A player with a hooligan reputation had found his true niche at a club then notorious for its barbarous followers and players' ill-discipline. But Howard Wilkinson saw much more to Jones than the pantomime villain image portrayed in tabloid newspapers. He was an accomplished exponent of the legitimate tackle; fit, brave, full of heart, with an unexpected range of footballing abilities.

Jones' move to Elland Road was a gamble for manager and player. Wilkinson had authority to buy his way out of the second division regardless of cost and the volatile Jones was, at £650,000, among the most expensive components in his re-vamped team. He coped in a way that surprised everyone, perhaps not least himself, making efforts that were largely successful to wrestle with his temperament; to avoid silly flare-ups. Wearing the number 4 shirt and operating mostly on the right side of midfield, Jones strove to show also he was capable of creative football; that the Wimbledon hoodlum had reformed.

The results of Vinnie Jones' efforts at artistry were mixed. On occasions, when he thought aloud in the popular press, he wondered if he was 'going soft'. Sometimes, his first touch let him down and he appeared cumbersome on the turn. Yet on other occasions Jones showed surprisingly adroit dribbling skills. He could also deliver long accurate passes, shoot with power and accuracy, and was alert to any goal-scoring possibility.

In 1989/90, Leeds' promotion season, Wilkinson relied much on the aerial bombardment of defences to gain his victories. Jones' ability to launch high teasing balls into the opposition penalty area from powerful throw-ins was an important element in this strategy which, while not especially pretty, brought Leeds United the Second Division Championship and deliverance from obscurity.

From the day he arrived, Vinnie Jones became a folk hero at Elland Road, still a macho icon if a disciplined team player. He never gave less than his best, and was worth much of his transfer fee for helping sustain the team's morale. Yet with Leeds' return to the first division, Wilkinson's treatment of Jones showed the manager to be as unsentimental as he was canny. A reorganised midfield based around the £1 million Gary McAllister placed a new emphasis on craft and technique. Vinnie, now no longer an automatic choice but demanding first team football, departed for Sheffield United. Jones had done his job for Leeds perfectly. His departure and the £750,000 Wilkinson obtained for him was, in all senses, a deal done on the best of terms.

BORN: Watford 5.1.65.
GAMES: 46 (2). GOALS: 5.
HONOURS: Second Division Championship 89/90.
OTHER CLUBS: Wimbledon 86/7-88/9 (77, 9);
Sheffield United 90/1-91/2 (35, 2);
Chelsea 91/2- (29, 2).

1989/90

CHRIS KAMARA

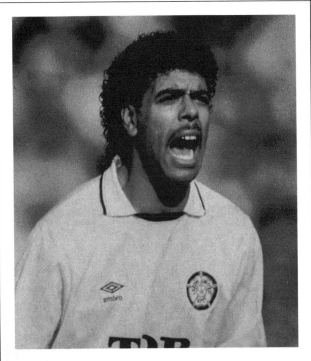

There are Leeds men who have made more appearances in a white shirt than Chris Kamara - he played less than a score of league matches - yet have created much less impact. Howard Wilkinson signed Kamara from Stoke City as a squad man to bolster Leeds' challenge for the second division title. To say that Kamara could add bite to midfield is an understatement: when roused, he bore down on opponents as if intent on devouring them alive.

Kamara was 32 when Wilkinson paid £150,000 for him but lacked nothing in speed, vigour or ambition. While occasionally his play when seeking to win the ball verged on the ferocious, he could strike choice long balls to change defence into attack, and combined his assorted talents to give a wonderful display in Leeds 4-0 demolition of Sheffield United when the two teams locked horns over the second division title.

Leeds fans liked not only his technical ability and hard running but also his commitment to the club. Many hoped to have seen more of him but in November 1990, while playing at Coventry, Kamara was stricken by the injury jinx that befell on Leeds left backs throughout the season. He hung on hoping for first team football before transferring to Luton in 1991/2. When he returned with them to Elland Road, Kamara produced an excellent combative performance and his reception from the home fans made clear the esteem in which his brief career at Elland Road was held.

BORN: Middlesbrough, 25.12.57. GAMES: 16 (7). GOALS: 1.
OTHER CLUBS: Portsmouth 75/6-76/7, 81/2 (74, 7);
Swindon Town 77/8-80/1, 85/6-87/8 (234, 27);
Brentford 81/2-84/5 (113, 28); Stoke City 88/9-89/90 (60, 5);
Luton Town 91/2- (27, 0).

1989/90 - 1991/92

GLYNN SNODIN

There are some in football who consider Glynn Snodin at least the equal of his younger, more fêted brother, Ian. Glynn's career at Leeds was interrupted by a lingering bout of glandular fever and injury but not before he had struck up an empathy with the Leeds fans. They appreciated his zest for the game and when he scored his occasional goals, he celebrated with a jubilant lack of inhibition, as if itching to get up on the terraces and join in the dancing.

The Snodin brothers spent five seasons playing in tandem for Doncaster Rovers, where Glynn made over 300 appearances, before he came to Leeds via Sheffield Wednesday for £150,000 in July 1987. He was a direct forceful player with ball-winning skills that could be used either in defence or midfield though sometimes games of attrition appeared to sap his strength.

Snodin was bought by Billy Bremner to play wide on the left in midfield but later deployed at left-back. A good technical player who appeared to have a surge of adrenalin when the ball was delivered to his feet, Snodin's forceful running and excellent crosses added to the Leeds attack. His left foot could also strike the ball with ferocious power; the sight of him squaring up to deliver a free kick within goal range caused jitters in many a defence. Glynn Snodin's career at Leeds was less fruitful than it might have been, but he is remembered fondly for his relish of the game and his good nature.

BORN: Rotherham, 14.2.60. GAMES: 96 (14). GOALS: 12.
OTHER CLUBS: Doncaster Rovers 76/7 (309, 61);
Sheffield Wednesday 85/6-87/8 (59, 1);
Oldham (on loan) 91/2 (6, 1); Rotherham United (non contract)
91/2 (2, 0); Heart of Midlothian 91/2 (4, 0).

1987/88 - 1990/91

JOHN HENDRIE

The career of John Hendrie at Leeds was a patchy, dislocated affair: one in which indifferent games alternated with displays of glistening brillliance. There were, of course, injuries that stopped Hendrie's flow, the first following a gruesome high tackle by Jon Gittens during the home game against Swindon Town in September 1989, where hitherto Hendrie had played a fine game, earning a penalty with a tricky run, then creating the second goal with a quick turn and volley that hit the crossbar.

In paying Newcastle United £600,000 for the winger's services, Howard Wilkinson was well aware of the ball-playing talent in which he was investing. But he had also bought with it an individ-ualistic temperament which perhaps was not apparent during Hendrie's finest days with Bradford City in the mid-1980s - where he had never suffered injuries - and where his wing play provided abundant goal-scoring ammunition for the gangling Ian Ormondroyd.

The Leeds management soon discovered Hendrie was an instinctive player, not to be governed by a game plan. While the Leeds United grand strategy did not preclude flair it did demand, above all, reliability and commitment. With Hendrie producing some of his wizardry in isolation, and giving the ball away more often than was good for the team effort, it became clear his future would not lie at Elland Road. More was expected of him than occasionally to illuminate a game and in June 1990, Wilkinson cut his losses by sellling Hendrie to Middlesbough for £550,000.

BORN: Lennoxtown, Strathclyde, 24.10.63.
GAMES: 24 (5) GOALS: 5.
OTHER CLUBS: Coventry City 81/2-83/4 (21, 2); Hereford
United *(on loan)* 83/4 (6, 0);
Bradford City 84/5-87/8 (173, 46); Middlesbrough 90/1 (76, 6).

1989/90

VINCE HILAIRE

As a creator of intricate patterns when on the ball, Vince Hilaire has had few equals. He was a player for whom there was no greater pleasure than to have the ball at his feet and embark on twisting, turning runs down the right wing. But when these could not be laid on for him, Hilaire cut a somewhat languid figure. Elsewhere on the pitch were areas of feverish, bruising activity that he tended to shun.

Hilaire, who arrived from Portsmouth with Noel Blake in the summer of 1988 at a cost of £190,000, was a genial entertainer on the field and a joker off it. He loved the game but his abundant talent was blunted by the lack of a mean streak. He had speed, sharpness, and mesmerising ball control but too often squandered the openings his abilities had created through a vague final pass or cross. Signs of concentrated application had been more evident in his Pompey days and their promotion season of 1986/7.

There are players whose innate skills survive the need for them also to battle in tight tough matches. Hilaire was not among them. A physical game, played at a high tempo, was not for Hilaire a source of pleasure; that he tolerated being passed by and was reluctant to forage for scraps in the thick of things prevented him being a winner at Leeds. But his party pieces were always worth coming to see.

BORN: Forest Hill, London, 10.10.59.
GAMES: 47 (3). GOALS: 7.
OTHER CLUBS: Crystal Palace 76/7-83/4 (255, 29);
Luton Town 84/5 (6, 0); Portsmouth 84/5-87/8 (146, 25);
Stoke City 89/90-90/1 (15, 3); Exeter City 91/2 (32, 4).

1988/89 - 1989/90

ANDY WILLIAMS

Among Howard Wilkinson's managerial talents is a knowledge of players who may seem less than obvious choices for the role he has in mind yet who do a sound job when assimilated into the team. Such was Wilkinson's first signing for Leeds: Andy Williams, a £175,000 buy from Rotherham United, an attacking right-sided midfielder little known outside Yorkshire, and unlikely to set pulses racing with high expectation.

However, enough was seen of Williams during Leeds' Second Division Championship season to regret his subsequent long absences through injury. While not a player of dazzling talent, Williams displayed good ball control, able to take on and beat defenders, considerable pace, a powerful shot and more ability in the air than the average midfield player.

Despite ill-luck with injuries, Williams was perhaps not quite of first division calibre. Although a hard worker, he was not especially combative and depended on others playing well around him if he were to be at his best. Injuries condemned him to obscurity as Leeds re-emerged as a first division force and when Williams recovered to seek first team football, he was sold to Notts County in March 1992.

BORN: Birmingham, 29.7.62.
GAMES: 30 (25). GOALS: 3.
OTHER CLUBS: Coventry City 85/6-86/7 (9, 0);
Rotherham United 86/7-88/9 (89, 13);
Port Vale *(on loan)* 91/2 (5, 0);
Notts County 91/2- (15, 1).

1988/89 - 1991/92

JOHN McCLELLAND

The euphemism mature instead of aged, sometimes employed by hopefuls in lonely hearts columns, could fairly be used by John McClelland, He was thirty-three when recruited by Howard Wilkinson in the summer of 1989, missed all but three of Leeds' games during the second division championship season of 1989-90, yet has refused to be put out to grass.

As cover for Chris Whyte, Chris Fairclough and the injured Peter Haddock, McClelland displayed the composure in central defence - though he could also play right-back - that had accrued through his years with, among others, Glasgow Rangers, Watford and Northern Ireland ; yet still had the legs to keep tabs on most opponents. Such was his positional sense and enthusiasm, McClelland might justifiably have been aggrieved at giving way to younger, fit-again colleagues.

Yet his debut for Leeds, during a 5-2 drubbing at Newcastle in which he was carrying a heel injury, was calamitous. McClelland's reappearance was in a triumphant 4-0 win over Sheffield United eight months later. In 1991/2, with Chris Fairclough injured, McClelland played splendidly in Leeds' early unbeaten run, with an energy that confounded opponents unwise enough to take him for an old crock.

BORN: Belfast, 7.12.55. GAMES: 26 (3). GOALS: 0.
HONOURS: 53 Northern Ireland Caps 1980-90.
OTHER CLUBS: Cardiff City 74/5 (4, 1); Bangor, Northern Ireland; Mansfield Town 79/80-80/1 (125, 8); Glasgow Rangers 81/2-84/5 (96, 4); Watford 84/85-88/9 *(on loan)* 89/90 (185, 3); Notts County *(on loan)* 91/2 (4, 0).

1989/90 -

MIKE WHITLOW

Mike Whitlows early football career was unpromising. Having joined Bolton Wanderers but failed to make the grade, he stepped down to the HFS Loans League with Witton Albion and worked as a labourer. Howard Wilkinson, however had been shadowing Whitlow and his partner at right-back, Neil Parsley, while managing Sheffield Wednesday.When he took over at Leeds, he was quick to bring both players to Elland Road in a £30,000 deal. Arriving in November 1988, Whitlow, wearing the number-7 shirt, made his league debut later that month in the 4-0 home victory over Stoke City.

It was, however at left back that Whitlow was to establish himself. In the first half of Leeds' promotion season, he showed a neat touch, good pace, and sound positional skills. At that time, Whitlow was an important component of a side playing fluid and effective football. But injury, then loss of confidence - he was prone to bouts of self-criticism - saw him surrender his position to Jim Beglin for most of the rest of the season after mid-February.

On Leeds' return to the first division, injuries bedevilled whomever wore the number 3 shirt, Whitlow included. But he was sufficiently versatile to make auxiliary performances in midfield when Peter Haddock was given a run at left-back. There, he looked comfortable on the ball and showed adequate skills but perhaps lacked the devil and self-belief to dictate play and make inspired contributions. In search of more regular first team football, he transferred to Leicester City in March 1992.

BORN: Northwich, Cheshire, 13.1.68.
GAMES: 66 (20). GOALS: 4.
OTHER CLUBS: Leicester City 91/92. (3, 0).

1988/89 - 1991/92

JIM BEGLIN

It would have been miraculous, and among the great transfer coups if, having acquired the injury-stricken Liverpool left-back Jim Beglin on a free transfer, Howard Wilkinson had benefited from his full recovery and Beglin had managed to reproduce week after week the composed performances that so caught the eye at Anfield in the mid 1980s.

Alas, it was not to be so, though the gamble was worth taking for manager and player. Irish-born Beglin, who had broken a leg while playing against Everton, failed to make a league appearance for Liverpool in either 1987/8 or 1988/9, and was never lucky enough to have an extended run in the Leeds team. Injury would ultimately defeat him, despite one or two false dawns, and force him out of the game.

For Beglin and for Leeds, it was cause for frustration and sorrow. In the few games he played and in training the Leeds management could see he was a fine player, albeit not fully fit; one with great balance, anticipation, well-schooled in the Liverpool tradition not only at defending but in playing football, passing and creating. Despite everyone's best efforts and spells on loan, the Beglin renaissance never came; problems with ligaments and arthritis curtailed a career that promised so much more.

BORN: Dublin, 29.7.63. GAMES: 18 (1). GOALS: 0.
HONOURS: Second Division Championship 89/90.
15 Republic of Ireland Caps 84-87.
OTHER CLUBS: Liverpool 84/5-86/7 (64, 2);
Plymouth Argyle *(on loan)* 90/1 (5, 0);
Blackburn Rovers *(on loan)* 90/1 (6, 0).

1989/90

IMRE VARADI

Some strikers are battlers with the mental and physical endurance to toil away every week in search of openings and half chances; others are walk-on acts, lacking perhaps the stamina and application for a full season's toil but with the cunning to disorientate a defence and score goals on occasional appearances.

Imre Varadi is a player of the latter kind for whom Leeds United is his seventh club. In the 1980s, he was a prolific scorer with Sheffield Wednesday and Newcastle and later Manchester City. Varadi is, like his recent predecessor Keith Edwards, blessed with an instinct for goal and the speed to match. At five feet eight, he is not dominant in the air but quick to feed off the turmoil created in defences by colleagues.

Varadi's appearances for Leeds have been limited and he has scored just four goals in 19 league games but his presence has often been sufficient to distract opposition defenders. Few, however, expected Varadi to build a long-term career at Elland Road and it was little surprise when he was loaned to Luton in March 1992.

BORN: Paddington, London, 8.7.59.
GAMES: 20 (3). GOALS: 4.
OTHER CLUBS: Sheffield United 78/9 (10, 4);
Everton 79/80-80/1 (26, 6);
Newcastle United 81/2-82/3 (81, 39);
Sheffield Wednesday 83/4-84/5, 88/9 (98, 36);
West Bromwich Albion 85/6 (32, 9);
Manchester City 86/7-88/9 (65, 26);
Luton Town *(on loan)* 91/2 (6, 1).

1989/90 -

PETER HADDOCK

That Peter Haddock was allowed to leave Newcastle United, for whom he made only 57 league appearances in five seasons, so cheaply somewhat mystified the Leeds management. But club politics and the calibre and form of colleagues may hold sway over a player's progress; as may proneness to injury. There is little doubt that Haddock, whose versatility in midfield and in defence was quickly appreciated at Leeds, would have played more than his 120 or so games for the Elland Road club were he less susceptible to getting hurt.

After his £45,000 move from Newcastle in June 1986, injury got Haddock's Leeds career got off to a false start. In 1990/1, a season in which defenders, especially left-backs, appeared cursed at Leeds, Haddock was afflicted with knee ligament trouble. But in the intervening three seasons, he was a steady regular player and had a distinguished campaign during Leeds' Second Division Championship season of 1989/90.

Haddock's preference is for the right side but his most accomplished games have been at the centre of the defence, as the man who covers rather than the one who launches himself for the first ball. Haddock is cool under pressure, capable of receiving the ball in tight spots then extricating himself and his team from difficulty.

Even at left-back, Haddock is quick enough to get the ball on to his better foot. Good pace and delicacy of touch also showed his fitness to play in midfield if called upon. Had he been more aggressive and less vulnerable, some stern and knowledgeable critics on the Elland Road staff feel Peter Haddock might have been fit for an England cap, let alone the first division.

BORN: Newcastle-upon-Tyne, 9.12.61.
GAMES 120 (16). GOALS: 1.
HONOURS: Second Division Championship 89/90.
OTHER CLUBS: Newcastle United 81/2-85/6 (57, 0);
Burnley *(on loan)* 85/6 (7, 0).

1986/87 -

VINCE BROCKIE

IAN ANDREWS

DYLAN KERR

VINCE BROCKIE 1987/88

Right-back. BORN: Greenock, 2.2.69.
GAMES: 2. GOALS: 0.
OTHER CLUBS: Doncaster Rovers 88/9-90/1 (54, 7).

RUSSELL DOIG 1986/87-1987/88

Winger. BORN: Millport, Scotland, 17.1.64.
GAMES: 5 (5). GOALS: 0.
OTHER CLUBS: East Stirling 83/4-85/6 (109, 9);
Peterborough United (on loan) 86/7 (7, 0);
Hartlepool United 87/8-89/90 (33, 1).

IAN ANDREWS 1988/89

Goalkeeper. BORN: Nottingham, 1.12.64.
GAMES: 1. GOALS: 0.
OTHER CLUBS: Leicester City 82/3-87/8 (119, 0);
Swindon Town (on loan) 83/4 (1, 0);
Glasgow Celtic 88/9 (5, 0); Southampton 90/1- (5, 0).

JIM MELROSE 1987/88

Forward. BORN: Glasgow 7.10.58. GAMES: 3 (3). GOALS: 0.
OTHER CLUBS: Partick Thistle 75/6-79/80 (122, 31);
Leicester City 80/1-82/3 (72, 21); Coventry City 82/3 (24, 8);
Glasgow Celtic 83/4 (29, 7); Wolverhampton Wanderers (on loan)
84/5 (7, 2); Manchester City 84/5-85/6 (34, 8);
Charlton Athletic 85/6-87/8 (48, 19);
Shrewsbury Town 87/8-89/90 (49, 3).

DYLAN KERR 1988/89 -

Midfield. BORN: Valetta, Malta, 14.1.67.
GAMES: 4 (5). GOALS: 0.
OTHER CLUBS: Doncaster Rovers (on loan) 91/2 (7, 1);
Blackpool (on loan) 91/2 (13, 1).

KEN DE MANGE 1987/88

Midfield. BORN: Dublin 3.9.64. GAMES: 17 (1). GOALS: 1.
HONOURS: 2 Republic of Ireland Caps 87-89. OTHER
CLUBS: Scunthorpe United (on loan from Liverpool) 86/7 (3, 2);
Hull City 87/8-90/1 (68, 2).

RUSSELL DOIG

JIM MELROSE

KEN de MANGE

CHRIS O'DONNELL

TONY AGANA

CHRIS TURNER

CHRIS O'DONNELL 1989/90

Defender. BORN: Newcastle-upon-Tyne, 26.5.68.
GAMES: 0 (1). GOALS: 0.
OTHER CLUBS: Ipswich Town 85/6-88/9 (14, 0);
Northampton Town *(on loan)* 87/8 (1, 0).

MICKEY THOMAS 1989/90

Midfield. BORN: Mochdre, New Colwyn Bay, Wales, 7.7.54.
GAMES: 3. GOALS: 0. HONOURS: 51 Wales Caps 1977-86.
OTHER CLUBS: Wrexham 71/2-78/9, 91/2- (252, 34);
Manchester United 78/9-80/1 (100, 11);
Everton 81/2 (10, 0); Brighton 81/2 (20, 0);
Stoke City 82/3-83/4 (57, 14);
Chelsea 83/4-84/5 (44, 9); West Bromwich Albion 85/6 (20, 0);
Derby County *(on loan)* 85/6 (9, 0);
Shrewsbury Town 88/9 (40, 1) Stoke City 89/90-90/1 (43, 7);
Wrexham 91/2- (27, 1).

TONY AGANA 1991/92

Striker. BORN: London 2.2.63. GAMES 1 (1) GOALS: 0.
OTHER CLUBS: Watford 87/8 (15, 1);
Sheffield United 87/8-91/2 (117, 41);
Notts County 91/2 (11, 1).

GARY KELLY 1991/92 -

Forward. BORN: Drogheda, Ireland, 9.7.74.
GAMES: 0 (3) GOALS: 0.

CHRIS TURNER 1989/90

Goalkeeper. BORN: Sheffield 15.9.58. GAMES: 2. GOALS: 0.
OTHER CLUBS: Sheffield Wednesday 76/7-78/9, 89/90 - (166, 0);
Lincoln City *(on loan)* 78/9 (5, 0);
Sunderland 79/80-84/5 (195, 0);
Manchester United 85/6-88/9 (64, 0);
Leyton Orient 91/2- (34, 0).

DAVID WETHERALL 1991/92

Defender. BORN: Shefffield 14.3.71.
GAMES 0 (1). GOALS: 0.

MICKEY THOMAS

GARY KELLY

DAVID WETHERALL

GORDON STRACHAN

Even though he had just turned 32, there was some surprise when, in March 1989, Gordon Strachan was considered surplus to Manchester United's requirements even though he was languishing in less than splendid isolation on the right wing. Howard Wilkinson used his persuasive powers to convince him there was a future in the second division with a decadent big-time club set on reviving its fortunes regardless of cost.

In his new life, the slight, red-haired Strachan, played a darting attacking game on the right side of midfield. Some Leeds fans with long memories made comparisons with Billy Bremner but Strachan's arrival also evoked echoes of other past glories and brilliant small midfield generals: of Bobby Collins and Johnny Giles, who had transferred from Manchester United in similar circumstances 26 years earlier.

Strachan, at £300,000, would prove the most brilliant purchase of Wilkinson's managerial career. He was quickly awarded the team captaincy. Gone were the lonely days he had known at Old Trafford: at Elland Road, Strachan became the focal point of all things creative, leading by example, cajoling any team-mate who showed signs of weakening when the going got rough.

Gordon Strachan may have lacked the toughness of Collins or Bremner's ferocious tackling. But his passing and shooting skills, his ability to read the game and switch the direction of play; and above all, his leadership qualities were priceless. It was always Strachan who would find a way through where none seemed likely; Strachan who could summon some wily skill in a crucial game when huffing and puffing had failed.

If his influence exceeded everyone's expectations, so did his durability. In the promotion season of 1989/90, Strachan played every league game; and made 104 successive appearances before a hip injury forced him out of the league game at Southampton on March 2 1991. Generally though, despite his unflinching involvement in the thick of the action, he was successful in avoiding injury until afflicted by sciatica in 1991/2. His fitness seemed age-defying: Strachan paid strict attention to his diet and, at 33, could still run 800 and 1,500 metres as quickly as seven years earlier.

Gordon Strachan was the finest buy made by any Leeds manager since Don Revie. In almost every game, good things flowed from his feet. For thousands of Manchester United fans, Strachan was a constant source of despair; sold for a song, then working miracles across the Pennines in an enemy camp during his prolonged Indian Summer.

BORN: Edinburgh, 9.2.57.
GAMES: 146 (1). GOALS: 32.
HONOURS: League Championship 91/2;
Second Division Championship 89/90.
50 Scotland Caps 80-92.
OTHER CLUBS: Dundee 74/5-76/7 (60, 13);
Aberdeen 77/8-83/4 (183, 55);
Manchester United 84/5-88/9 (160, 33).

1988/89 -

LEE CHAPMAN

To miss what seems like an easy goal, you have to get into a scoring position in the first place. There weren't many other players out there who missed. Thus Howard Wilkinson's laconic observations to the assembled press after Lee Chapman squandered an easy chance during a 0-0 draw against West Ham in March 1992 as Leeds' challenge for the league title became edgier and more ragged.

Chapman is a player by whom Wilkinson will always stand. And as each season passes at Elland Road, Lee Chapman has come to be held in higher public esteem. When first signed, in January 1990, he was not hailed as a marvellous buy; grudging references were made to him being awkward but effective. By the end of the campaign, Chapman had provided for Leeds their most treasured moment since Allan Clarke's stooping header won the FA Cup 18 years earlier: the goal at Bournemouth that finally delivered Leeds from a second division that could contain them no longer.

Hitherto, Chapman had wandered around a handful of first division clubs, sometimes successfully, at other times to no great end. He was 30 when he arrived at Leeds from Nottingham Forest for £400,000 and there was little to suppose he might become a pillar on which Leeds would be able to lean. That he did says much for the chemistry between player and management and a system in which Chapman's intelligence and willingness to run could be exploited. Howard Wilkinson has a way with his Sheffield Wednesday old boys.

Chapman marked his arrival with a goal in a 2-1 victory at Blackburn Rovers. Thereafter, goals issued from him steadily as Leeds hit the front of the second division and summoned all their nerve and know-how to stay there. But the following season, against first division defences, would not his ungainly style, his apparent lack of class, be exposed? Chapman answered the doubters by finishing as the division's top scorer in all competitions.

He has shown remarkable stamina, both in pursuing balls knocked over his head so he can hold up play, and when making rapid ground with his somewhat jerky, stooping run to send goalwards high crosses with his head or low ones with his boot. Chapman is conspicuously brave, and having nose-dived into the cinder track during a game at Tottenham in February 1991, was raring to present his scarred face to first division defences long before he was fully fit.

When he broke his wrist during the Rumbelows League Cup battle against Manchester United during 1991/2, it was, of course, in a goal-mouth challenge: Chapman, getting in where it hurt. Without him, Leeds faltered, yet team-mates still knocked high balls forward as if hoping their centre-forward's apparition might descend from the sky to soak up punishment or create something out of nothing.

BORN: Lincoln, 5.12.59. GAMES: 116. GOALS: 60.
HONOURS: League Championship 91/2; Second Division Championship 89/90.
OTHER CLUBS: Plymouth Argyle (on loan) 78/9 (4, 0); Stoke City 79/80-81/2 (99, 34);
Arsenal 82/3-83/4 (23, 4); Sunderland 83/4 (15, 3);
Sheffield Wednesday 84/5-87/8 (149, 63); Niort, France;
Nottingham Forest 88/9-89/90 (48, 15).

1989/90 -

CHRIS WHYTE

Few contemporary central defenders are more reassuring figures than Chris Whyte. Yet he has come to prominence along the low road, after a career that promised much at Arsenal in the early 1980s disintegrated when he lost form. Instead of a possible England place, there beckoned instead a spell in Los Angeles then two seasons with West Bromwich Albion, a club guaranteed to give any footballer a variegated career of ups and downs.

But once at West Bromwich, Whyte's self-assurance and solidity were restored. Watching him after his £500,000 move to Leeds at the start of 1990/1 as he dominated in the air and positioned himself wisely to intercept menacing passes, it is hard to imagine him ever struggling. For the loose-limbed Whyte has performed with great authority, fending off attackers who snap at his heels with near disdain, and playing with a sense of enjoyment though without compromising his will to win.

As a defender, Whyte is a man for the stern tackle and clearing his lines without ceremony. When he ventures forward, another side of his footballing character takes over, an urge to produce fancy footwork and beat players one after the other. For a big man, Whyte shows a surprisingly delicate touch and experienced defences have been caught out, Manchester United's and Wimbledon's among them. Chris Whyte as ball player and sharpshooter is less fanciful than it may sound.

In his two years at Leeds, the amiable Whyte has played the best football of his career and though rarely spoken of as a contender for England, it would be understandable if, on occasions, he has looked around, puzzled, and wondered who in the league has outshone him.

BORN: London 2.9.61. GAMES: 96. GOALS: 5.
HONOURS: League Championship 91/2.
OTHER CLUBS: Arsenal 81/2-85/6 (90 ,8); Crystal Palace *(on loan)* 84/5 (13, 0);
Los Angeles USA (Indoor League); West Bromwich Albion 88/9-89/90 (84, 7).

1990/91 -

CHRIS FAIRCLOUGH

Chris Fairclough is among the least demonstrative of footballers. His perfomances are, perhaps, for connoisseurs who rather than follow star players that easily catch the eye prefer to study the man at the back clearing his lines and tidying up loose ends.

Fairclough has been the epitome of tidiness at the centre of the Leeds defence since being signed from Tottenham before the transfer deadline of 1988/9. During 1989/90 he excelled both in defence, where he was composed, speedy and mobile, and as an auxiliary attacker when he displayed good anticipation and bravery. He was a worthy supporters' Player of the Year.

Indeed, several of Fairclough's forays into opposition penalty areas proved crucial: his forceful equaliser in the 1-1 home draw against Blackburn Rovers early in the season; his goal against Watford that set up a 2-1 home win in November, for which he had to kneel down amid thrashing bodies and flailing boots to get in his header.

Fairclough brought with him good footballing habits learned from Nottingham Forest and Tottenham, both clubs that usually look for more in a defender than the knack of crunching strikers. Besides his crisp tackling, Fairclough has the technique to play good balls out of defence. If, in a team of assertive personalities such as Strachan, Batty and Sterland, he seems a subdued figure, flashes of temper displayed when he is provoked hint at passions simmering beneath an impassive facade.

Save for an occasional tendency to get dragged out of position, Chris Fairclough, playing in concert with Chris Whyte, has been consistent and reliable. Often during a game, Fairclough's has been the contribution hardest to remember. Then, on reflection, you realise it is because he never put a foot wrong.

BORN: Nottingham 12.4.64. GAMES: 136 (3). GOALS: 16.
HONOURS: League Championship 91/2; Second Division Championship 89/90.
OTHER CLUBS: Nottingham Forest 82/3-86/7 (107, 1);
Tottenham Hotspur 87/8-88/9 (60, 5).

1988/89 -

DAVID BATTY

When David Batty burst on to the scene, he was, for Leeds fans something they had lacked for a generation: a player born among them with fire, talent and drive who wanted to play, above all, for Leeds United, the club he had supported in his childhood. For years, fans had cast around for heroes but Eddie Gray's home-grown candidates had spread their wings elsewhere and assorted imports were often frail and vulnerable idols.

In his early games - Batty made his debut in November 1987 as an 18-year-old during a 4-2 home win over Swindon Town - he may have looked like a cocky, even belligerent, small boy. But opponents who anticipated he would be easy to push around discovered instead that Batty did the hustling; that it was Batty who charged in with tackles fierce enough to knock the stuffing out of bigger and older men.

As a determined, sometimes ruthless forager after the ball in midfield, Leeds fans had not seen his like since Brian Flynn, though it was with Billy Bremner that fond comparisons started to be made. The tenacity, the passion, the necessary mean streak, the capacity for future leadership were all there though Batty, now an established England player, has yet to show Bremner's capacity for brilliant improvisation and scoring goals.

The paucity of Batty's goals is a cause célèbre at Elland Road. It is not that he lacks shooting power: his rare scoring strikes have had plenty of vim. He has sometimes lacked luck and so his self-confidence as a marksman has been eroded. But that has not deterred Batty from conducting business as usual elsewhere, breaking up the rhythm of opponents, then winning the ball to build up constructive attacking moves.

There are no apathetic performances from David Batty. On a bad day, he may find it hard to rise above a congested midfield scrap and his distribution becomes erratic. Yet few players are more willing or adept than he at chasing back to retrieve something from their own mistakes. He can be a thrilling sight when in the mood to burst forward from midfield and bear down on goal leaving his opponents standing as he did in creating a wonderful goal for Lee Chapman during the glorious 4-5 home defeat by Liverpool in April 1991.

It is this side to his game of which managers and fans would love to see more. Batty, at 23, veteran of almost 200 games for Leeds is still maturing and discovering his game. A legend may yet be in the making.

BORN: Leeds, 2.12.68.
GAMES: 187 (9). GOALS: 3.
HONOURS: League Championship 91/2;
Second Division Championship 89/90.
8 England Caps 91-92.

1987/88 -

GARY McALLISTER

Gary McAllister, the most stylish and complete midfielder Leeds had had for more than a decade, was nearly the source of the club's greatest grief. In the battle of nerves that became United's run-in for the 1990 Second Division Championship, his equalising strike for Leicester City in Leeds' penultimate match brought with it a terrible haunting fear of last gasp failure.

A late winner by Gordon Strachan during a match of excruciating tension brought relief from McAllister and his wiles. His midfield skills for Leicester had been outstanding in the 1989/90 season and had alerted among others, the omnivorous Liverpool. But when he became available, Howard Wilkinson moved swiftly to convince McAllister of Leeds United's ambition; that a player of his class had a future with the newly-promoted Yorkshire club. The acquisition of McAllister was a statement of intent by Wilkinson: that Leeds United intended to contest the first division on skill allied to the hustling long ball game that characterised their muscular campaign to escape division two.

As Gary McAllister arrived, Vinnie Jones, symbol of the previous toiling season gave way; and there was an emphatic shift towards a more stylish approach through the midfield quartet of Strachan, Batty, McAllister and Speed. The lean McAllister looked as if he could have belonged to an earlier, more austere football era, with his short brushed-back hair, a hint of sideburn and gaunt face.

His ability had already been recognised by Scotland at international level. Operating from the left side of midfield, here was a player with great positional sense, whose skill at making time and distributing the most intelligent ball imaginable recalled Johnny Giles. His powerful forward runs and accurate shooting, though providing surprisingly few goals, added a further dimension to United's attack. After a diffident start to the 1990/1 season, in which he tended to be overshadowed by Strachan, McAllister grew in confidence, stature, and fitness. It became clear that for £1 million, Howard Wilkinson had found excellent value.

BORN: Motherwell, 25.12.64.
GAMES: 97 (1). GOALS: 10.
HONOURS: League Championship 91/2.
12 Scotland Caps 90-92.
OTHER CLUBS: Motherwell 81/2-85/6 (59, 6);
Leicester City 85/6-89/90 (201, 47).

1990/91 -

ROD WALLACE

During a 2-0 defeat at Southampton in March 1991, one of Leeds' rare turgid displays since returning to the first division, the vistitors' defence was tortured by Rod Wallace. His speed off the mark caused panic, his scampering runs left defenders strewn behind him.

By the summer, along with his twin brother Ray, he had become a Leeds United player at a cost of £1.6 million. There was excitement at Rod Wallace's coming, and perhaps relief that he would not be tormenting the Leeds rearguard in future. While Ray has yet to play a Leeds first team game, by mid-term 1991/2, Rod's eye was in and he was making other defences suffer with his electrifying quickness, adroit close control and the energy to dart up and down both flanks of the field.

When finding or making space to embark on shimmering goalwards runs, there are few more exhilarating sights in football and Wallace is quite uncontainable. He had a splendid time during Leeds' 6-1 plundering of flu-stricken Sheffield Wednesday in January 1992 but his individual contribution has rarely had more impact than in the 1-0 home win over Everton the previous November. With Leeds down to ten men after Chris Fairclough was sent off, Wallace roamed the pitch, kept Everton on edge and, as time dripped away, showed marvellous athleticism to hook in the winner from a right wing cross whipped over to the far post.

Players of Wallace's type do not deliver supercharged performances all the time. Some days, his exuberance and appetite for bold runs on goal desert him, and his deft flicks go astray. But in the mood, Rod Wallace is potent attacker who should have a great future; one who, when on song, is worth whatever you paid to watch him. His goal to celebrate Leeds winning the League Championship in the final game of 1991/2 against Norwich, when he darted past four defenders before scoring with a low cross shot, was vivid footballing theatre.

BORN: Lewisham, London, 2.10.69.
GAMES: 38 GOALS 13.
HONOURS: League Championship 91/2.
OTHER CLUBS: Southampton 87/8-90/1 (128, 45).

1991/92 -

GARY SPEED

Gary Speed's principal weakness is his failure to realise quite how good a player he is. Thus the view of Howard Wilkinson, who has stuck with the young Welsh international even when form and confidence have temporarily deserted him, and voted him player of the year during the League Championship season.

Although Speed prefers playing a more central role, he has been used on the left side as an attacking midfield player. Speed's great qualities are his pace and mobility, a willingness to run until he drops, the ability to win balls in the air with superbly-timed athletic leaps, and a sharp eye for goal.

With these qualities and an eagerness to learn the game Gary Speed, who exudes an air of shyness despite having attained pin-up status, has been stretched to the limits by his manager. Towards the end of 1991/2, with Tony Dorigo injured, Speed was deployed at left-back; a clear sign of Wilkinson's determination to exploit every ounce of his versatility.

Speed has had some fine moments as a goal-scorer, being particularly adept at losing markers at set pieces and timing runs on goal to meet high cross balls. Despite the lack of self-belief to which he is prone, he has, even as a newcomer, shown a cool head at times of frenetic excitement, such as when running almost the length of the pitch to score Leeds' fourth goal against Sheffield United in the Second Division Championship battle of April 1990.

On off days, Speed has played with his usual endeavour but also a slight agitation when his passes, usually of high quality, have found opponents more often than team-mates. His future at the highest level though looks assured; still only in his early 20s, there are many who await with keen interest Gary Speed's maturity - and the discovery of his best position.

BORN: Mancot, North Wales, 8.6.69.
GAMES: 107 (16). GOALS: 23.
HONOURS: League Championship 91/2;
Second Division Championship 89/90.
14 Wales Caps 90-92.

1988/89 -

MEL STERLAND

Another expensive component of Howard Wilkinson's lavishly reconstructed Leeds United team, Mel Sterland may have wondered what the future held as he departed Scottish league champions Glasgow Rangers - he had been there just four months but long enough to win a Championship medal - for English second division football.

The key, once again, was the relationship between manager and player. Wilkinson, in paying £600,000 for Sterland, knew precisely what he was getting, having managed him at Sheffield Wednesday for whom Sterland had signed as an 18-year-old in 1979.
He made a forceful contribution to Wednesday's promotion in 1984 under Wilkinson's management and spent most of the 1980s at or near the top of his trade, winning his one full England cap against Saudi Arabia in November 1988.

Sterland's sojourn in Scotland was brief - he left Wednesday in March 1989 and was back in Yorkshire, at Leeds, by July. Vigour and honesty have characterised his performances for the club. Sterland is a right-back who looks to attack with surging runs down the flank.
He is a strong tackler whose performances are rarely less than robust; a key figure in Leeds United's promotion season founded on fitness and hard graft.

Sterland is also an accomplished practitioner of the long throw-in, a favourite Wilkinson device for causing tremors in the opposition penalty area. And he can shoot with ferocity; his ability to blast the ball from free kicks has yielded several crucial goals and earned him the nickname Zico, although perhaps he is unable to bend a football with quite the same wicked deviousness as the Brazilian maestro.

If Sterland has a weakness, it is when exposed to swift-running flank players. Then his lack of great pace becomes noticeable, leaving him to flounder in the wake of darting wingers, especially when pulled out of position by his attacking instincts. But overall, the genial Sterland's contributions have given Leeds United much of their new-found impetus. Once again, Wilkinson had found good value at a high price.

BORN: Sheffield, 1.10.61.
GAMES: 129 (2). GOALS: 18.
HONOURS: League Championship 91/2;
Second Division Championship 89/90.
1 England Cap 1988.
OTHER CLUBS: Sheffield Wednesday 78/9-88/9 (279, 37);
Glasgow Rangers 89/89 (9, 3).

1989/90 -

STEVE HODGE

Anyone recalling his vigorous skilful performances for England in the later stages of the 1986 World Cup could not doubt the calibre of Steve Hodge, even though his form since has sometimes been inconsistent, notably during an unsettled two seasons with Tottenham Hotspur.

Hodge is an attacking midfielder with the strength to win the ball and the technique then to use it wisely. He was bought by Howard Wilkinson for £900,000 from Nottingham Forest in summer 1991 to add depth to Leeds' already accomplished midfield, and early in the season was deployed as a substitute to help pep things up later in the game.

Steve Hodge has had his frustrations in being unable to break into the first team when Leeds hit some of their best form in mid-season 1991/2, and in suffering injury. Yet when picked, Hodge has made his mark, stepping up the tempo in midfield and bursting into the penalty area to score important goals, none perhaps more memorable than that which sunk Liverpool at Elland Road on September 21 - it was Hodge's first full league game in Leeds colours and gave his team an immense psychological fillip.

Hodge has a striker's instinct around the penalty area, a fierce shot, and the gift of slipping defenders at free kicks or when crosses are made that is always likely to yield goals. He will be hoping for more settled times and the chance to show the Leeds fans that he is still made of top quality stuff.

BORN: Nottingham, 25.10.62. GAMES: 16 (13). GOALS 7.
HONOURS: League Championship 91/2.
24 England Caps 1986-91.
OTHER CLUBS: Nottingham Forest 81/2-85/6, 88/9-90/1 (205, 50);
Aston Villa 85/6-86/7 (53, 12); Tottenham Hotspur 86/7-87/8 (45, 7).

1991/92 -

Injuries struck down left-backs so regularly in the 1990/91 season that it seemed as if some malign fate were intervening at Leeds. If the prospect of joining a club as overtly ambitious as any in the league lured Tony Dorigo to Elland Road from Chelsea in summer 1991, he could be forgiven any qualms about his chances of surviving intact.

Australian-born Dorigo epitomises the complete modern defender: an all-round footballer who happens to play at the back. Tony Dorigo emphasised Howard Wilkinson's desire to aim as high as possible and a new era in which England internationals at their peak were being imported to Elland Road.

Chelsea fans felt the loss of Tony Dorigo savagely: a cry of 'Judas' greeted his return in a Leeds shirt. Footballers such as Dorigo, with their range of abilities and assured presence, are not easily replaced. His style is to defend by anticipating danger and making timely interventions: Dorigo cuts almost a dapper figure yet when called on is as capable a last-ditch defender as any, with the pace to catch up enemy strikers who have broken free before making a crisp, precise tackle.

Although versatile, Tony Dorigo is less comfortable when occasionally deployed at right-back. The left is Dorigo's favoured side, from where he revels in thrusting forward with darting direct runs or overlapping on the flank to deliver teasing crosses. He can receive the ball under pressure then deliver short neat passes or long raking balls that suddenly put his team on the offensive. And his booming left-foot shot is an excellent weapon to have in the armoury: a Dorigo special whizzing goalwards from 25 yards or so is a joy for Leeds fans to behold.

BORN: Melbourne, Australia, 31.12.65. GAMES: 44. GOALS: 3.
HONOURS: League Championship 91/2.
10 England Caps 90-92.
OTHER CLUBS: Aston Villa 83/4-86/7 (111, 1);
Chelsea 87/8-90/1 (146, 11).

1991/92 -

CARL SHUTT

There are some players with whom the toil of regular first team football seems to disagree yet who flourish as a support act. Striker Carl Shutt, a relative late-comer to league football at the age of 23 when he joined Sheffield Wednesday from Spalding in May 1985, is among them. While he lacks the qualities and endurance to soak up pressure and create chances at the front-line week in, week out, he has the striker's nostrils that twitch at the scent of a goal chance.

Shutt seems happier and more secure as a late comer-on when he can inflict his damage on opposition defences. In almost half his 25 appearances during 1990/91, he was either taken off or came on as substitute. However, his full debut for Leeds - Shutt is one for producing his fireworks in short bursts - produced a hat trick against Bournemouth in April 1989.

Since then Shutt, who is mobile and good in the air though sometimes seems to lack the sharpness of a top drawer striker, has made timely interventions on goal. He can, intuitively, take up good positions and finish crisply; and if not one of the great battlers, he is always liable to punish unwary defences.

BORN: Sheffield 10.10.61. GAMES: 51 (32). GOALS: 19.
HONOURS: League Championship 91/2.
OTHER CLUBS: Sheffield Wednesday 85/6-87/8 (40, 16);
Bristol City 87/8-88/9 (66, 10).

1988/89 -

JON NEWSOME

Injury to Mel Sterland forced Howard Wilkinson to make some uncomfortable experiments at right-back before he decided to entrust the slot to young Jon Newsome. Rarely will a player with minimal league experience face a greater test of his temperament than being asked to buttress a team seeking its first League Championship for 18 years. Newsome responded superbly.

He will, of course, be remembered for two vital goals: the one in only his second league match that thrust Leeds into the lead at Tottenham in March; the other, his celebrated diving header at Sheffield United that brought the title within Leeds' grasp. But no less crucial was some of Newsome's defensive work in the tumultuous final weeks of the championship race, not least his wonderful tackle to recover the ball from Ian Rush in the 0-0 draw at Anfield when Rush, one of the world's great strikers appeared to have the goal at his mercy.

If occasionally Newsome has looked a little uncertain when in possession, it should be remembered that when the stakes were at their highest, he never let Leeds down. His nerve has passed the sternest of examinations and, with some technical improvement, he could become a great defensive prospect.

BORN: Sheffield, 6.9.70. GAMES: 6 (3). GOALS: 2.
HONOURS: League Championship 91/2.
OTHER CLUBS: Sheffield Wednesday 89/90-90/1 (7, 0).

1991/92 -

ERIC CANTONA

That a capricious and reputedly ill-tempered - albeit highly gifted - Frenchman might bolster Leeds United's challenge for the first division title in 1991/2 seems fanciful. With Lee Chapman injured, the name of almost every credible target man in the first division was bandied about as a possible replacement. Howard Wilkinson showed boldness and originality in opting for Eric Cantona instead.

.Cantona was big, beefy and brilliant; a leading light in a distinguished French national side. But he also lacked self-control. Howard Wilkinson, under whom no player has yet rocked the boat at Elland Road, was undeterred. In February 1992, Cantona, who at that time spoke almost no English, joined Leeds on loan from Nîmes.

Once fit to withstand the rigours of the English league, Cantona displayed enough brilliance to justify Wilkinson's gamble. In an otherwise frustrating 0-0 draw at home to West Ham in March 1992, Cantona made everyone else look ordinary as he showed, by turns, extraordinary power and control in his running, measured delicacy in his flick-ons and the wit to throw defenders with cunning back-heeled passes. His goal that finished off Chelsea two weeks later, a chest trap, flick and volley, had spectators gasping at its brilliance. All this and self-discipline too. No-one could have asked more of an *enfant terrible*.

BORN: France, 24.5.66. GAMES: 6 (9). GOALS: 3.
HONOURS: League Championship 91/2.
OTHER CLUBS: Auxerre, Martigues, Marseille, Bordeaux *(on loan)*;
Montpelier *(on loan)*; Nîmes, (all France).

1991/92 -

DON REVIE

With the ascent to management of Don Revie, the 40 previous years of Leeds United's history became partially eclipsed. To have fantasies about creating one of Europe's greatest club sides from the husk of a debt-ridden club heading for the third division is one thing. That Revie went out and did it in less than 10 years is among soccer management's most monumental feats.

Revie had been absorbed by soccer tactics as a teenager, ever since lapping up Bill Sanderson's sophisticated talk-ins for the Middlesbrough Swifts. Permutations of the so-called deep Revie plan that brought success to Manchester City in the 1950s took up many pages of his early memoir, Soccer's Happy Wanderer. There was much reflection on the state of the game in general. Although he was only 33 when he became manager of Leeds in March 1961, the gestation period had been a long one.

An extraordinary combination of qualities was needed to revive Leeds United. Money, too, and Revie had the ear and the financial backing of Harry Reynolds, Leeds' millionaire chairman. Yet success was not instant. In Revie's second season, the third, not the first division loomed; he had a surfeit of moderate senior players and youthful talent too raw to face the weekly rigours of league football. His first inspirational signing, the veteran Bobby Collins, was the catalyst for change, and almost certainly spared Leeds relegation.

During 1962/3, the first shoots of new growth appeared. Revie drafted his protégés, rock solid youngsters such as Paul Reaney and Norman Hunter into the team. Billy Bremner had already established himself. Behind the scenes was taking place a revolution created by Revie's iron will and his meticulous attention to detail, his endless capacity for hard work, an aura of paternalism and discipline that led almost everyone at Elland Road to regard him with awe.

Revie was a clean, constructive and stylish player, never associated with ruthlessness until he became manager. But in the early days, only winning seemed to matter. There was a mean, hustling, streak running through Don Revie's sides that opponents, officials and spectators found tiresome. The Second Division Championship season of 1963/4 and the quest for the League and FA Cup double a year later were peppered with lurid, ferocious encounters.

The 'Dirty Leeds' tag stuck. So, for several years, did the club's inability to win major honours. Revie's organisational skills were without parallel, his eye for a fine young player unsurpassed, but a brooding, superstitious nature and a pathological caution that led him to overestimate mediocre opponents and inhibit his players may have stood between Leeds and a clutch of trophies. From 1968 to 1974 they won two League Championships, the FA Cup, the League Cup and the Inter Cities Fairs Cup twice, yet will forever be remembered for their failures at the death.

The Revie legacy is an extraordinary one. When, belatedly, he allowed his team of abundant talent to play with more freedom in the early 1970s, it was a class apart. There never was, and probably never will be, a better club team in Britain: subtle, fluid, ingenious yet still vigorous and, by 1971/2 quite irresistible. Yet in any abrasive encounter, critics scrambled to recall Leeds' past. Almost no-one, save Leeds partisans, loved them. Having mastered the art of winning, Revie craved the acclaim that had been bestowed on Manchester United and Real Madrid. But there were too many dark patches in the club's history, too much a sense that Revie the brilliant tactician was also a cynical manipulator.

Revie's succession to the job of England manager in 1974, in which, unlike at Leeds he was subject to forces beyond his control, was never marked by the same success. His sure touch seemed to desert him; he capped a posse of unsuitable players and, in trying to arrange commercial deals to benefit the players, was accused of being obsessed with money. Results went against him and Revie - for whom his days managing England had exacerbated a sense of paranoia and made him convinced the sack was round the corner - cooked up his escape route via a secret and lucrative deal to manage in the United Arab Emirates.

The disgrace that befell Revie when the story appeared in the Daily Mail before FA officials were informed was compounded by a series of articles in the Daily Mirror claiming he had attempted to bribe opponents to help throw key matches in Leeds United's favour. During his exile Revie's reputation never fully recovered, though his passing was still mourned at Leeds - where on his return he had a paid role as consultant - as successive managers failed to reproduce Revie's triumphant days.

He spent his latter years in an active semi-retirement, playing golf and helping his son Duncan's sports promotions business, before falling victim to motor-neurone disease in 1986, and enduring a desperate and lingering descent into paralysis before his death in Scotland on May 26 1989.

MANAGER: MARCH 1961 - JULY 1974

BRIAN CLOUGH

Like some turbulent priest, Brian Clough descended on Elland Road determined to drive out the spirit of Don Revie and all his works.

For the fact that his new team had just won the League Championship and played some football of extraordinary brilliance, he seemed to care nothing. Instead, he told the Leeds players at their first team talk they had won all their medals by cheating.

There was a history of highly-charged bruising encounters between Clough's former club, Derby County, and Leeds. The previous season, 1973/4, Clough had been moved to make a noisy public con-demnation of Revie's men. They were a team that had aged collectively, which, at the end of 1972/3, some critics suggested was ripe for the breaker's yard. Brian Clough, who had no sentimental attachment to Revie's sons, seemed raring to be the demolition foreman.

He imported, by Leeds standards, players of moderate ability: John O'Hare and John McGovern, Derby old boys, besides Duncan McKenzie from Nottingham Forest, and thrust them into the team. Clough's position at Leeds soon started to be undermined by poor results: just one victory in the first five games of the season. Deliberately or otherwise, he antagonised several senior professionals but despite his bluster felt insecure without his long-standing partner Peter Taylor on whom to lean.

Some players at Leeds felt Clough should have been given more of a chance. Others felt differently and said so during an extraor-dinary gathering called by uneasy directors to gauge their feelings about the new manager and his operations. Shortly after, an emergency board meeting was held and Clough was sacked: 44 days of turmoil and upheaval had cost the club dearly but left the former Derby manager financially secure - thanks to an estimated £200,000 pay off - albeit with a wounded ego. Those who expressed misgivings about Clough's summary dismissal might now look at his record since with Nottingham Forest and say 'I told you so'.

MANAGER: JULY - SEPTEMBER 1974

JIMMY ARMFIELD

A European Cup Final, an FA Cup semi-final and a League Cup semi-final within three seasons, yet Jimmy Armfield, Brian Clough's benign successor at Elland Road, was deemed to have failed. In four years, he had, without rancour, moved aside Revie's great players and made honourable attempts to build a new team that might compete at the top.

At first Armfield, who had learned the management trade at Bolton and over whose appointment the Leeds board deliberated, was valuable as a healer. After the 1975 European Cup Final he started to dismantle the ageing team and, aware of the chasm he would have to fill following the departure of Johnny Giles, brought to Leeds Tony Currie who remains among the most enthralling of the post-Revie players.

Yet with Armfield's reasonableness and good temper, there was a detectable lack of passion about the club, a feeling that the days at the top were ebbing away. There were times when Armfield's hand appeared too relaxed, occasioning a joke among the players that the manager's indecision was final. He bought good but not great players, and there was little of top quality coming through the junior ranks. Leeds United's consistency had gone.

At the end of 1978, the scale of Leeds' defeat by Nottingham Forest over two legs of the League Cup semi-final and ninth place in the League emphasised that the club was falling behind the élite. Don Revie had left behind an immense burden of expectation on his successors. Armfield's best was not quite good enough and he was dismissed after the end of the season.

MANAGER: OCTOBER 1974 - JULY 1978

JOCK STEIN

The appointment of Jock Stein as manager at Leeds seemed to satisfy a craving at the club and among supporters for someone of whom to be in awe once again. Brian Clough had been a rogue appointment; Jimmy Armfield had faded away. Stein had done incomparably great things with Celtic and extravagant hopes were pinned on the big man for more of the same.

Stein had been moved sideways, to the position of general manager at Celtic, after a road accident and a series of major operations. While Leeds presented him with a great opportunity to return to the thick of things, when the call came from his country to replace Ally Macleod as national team manager, Stein found it irresistible.

The fact that Stein, who was welcomed so heartily at Elland Road and stimulated such high expectations lasted just 44 days - precisely the same time as Brian Clough - is relished by those who collect ironies as well as statistics. It is impossible to know what he might have made of the job; there was no wholesale shake-up of the team Jimmy Armfield left behind and results in the first few weeks of 1978/9 were patchy. When Stein was lured back to Scotland to manage the national team, he left behind a Leeds public bemused and saddened. His appointment had been the great experiment that never was. Stein retained the job he had coveted for almost eight years before he collapsed and died after Scotland's tense World Cup qualifier against Wales on the night of September 10 1985.

MANAGER: AUGUST - OCTOBER 1978

JIMMY ADAMSON

After the trauma caused by Jock Stein's rapid coming and going, stability was needed once more at Elland Road. Jimmy Adamson's reign at Elland Road was to start with promise, yet by the end of his two year tenure, he had become the most reviled Leeds manager in modern times.

Adamson - like Jimmy Armfield, a somewhat avuncular figure - took over in October 1978, having failed to save Sunderland from relegation in 1976/7. Leeds tightened up considerably enjoying, from November to March 1979, a run of 16 games without defeat. The team finished fifth - high enough to resume campaigning in Europe - and reached the semi-finals of the League Cup once more.

With the wisdom of hindsight, there were ominous signs of harder times around the corner; not least the dismaying ease with which champions Liverpool pushed Leeds aside during their 3-0 win at Elland Road in the final game of 78-9. The next season, with Adamson having sold Tony Currie and Frank Gray, the midfield heart no longer beat with flair and colour, and Leeds won just four of their first 17 league games, a famine the like of which fans had not known for almost twenty years.

The unexpected flowering of teenage striker Terry Connor provided Adamson and the fans with some respite but too often the team looked ordinary, or worse. Supporters called for Adamson to be sacked after an abysmal 0-0 home draw with Coventry in March 1980. Attendances were now regularly below 20,000 and a wretched start to the new season brought calls for his head to a crescendo. Adamson had soaked up much abuse before resigning in Setember 1980 from what would be his last full-time job in soccer. In his wake, survival rather than cups and Championships became a preoccupation at Elland Road.

ALLAN CLARKE

There was much goodwill surrounding Allan Clarke's succession to the job of Leeds manager. He was a Revie old boy, a link with the glory days, scorer of the goal that brought about Leeds' solitary precious FA Cup Final victory. He also, a little self-consciously perhaps, acted out the managerial role with a brusque 'I'm-in-charge manner'.

But Clarke was not all talk. He had been conspicuously successful in reviving Barnsley's fortunes, gaining promotion then establishing the club as a force in the third division. No-one disbelieved him when he said he was a winner. He always had been.

There was rot to be stopped at Elland Road and Clarke, concentrating on defence, began by preventing Leeds handing out points to the rest of division one. But goals and midfield inspiration were pitifully lacking. In 1980/81 Leeds fans saw their team survive quite comfortably but they had to endure a diet of hard tack in the process.

In the first game of the following season, the Leeds defence was mauled as a newly-promoted and rampant Swansea City beat them 5-1. Some feel the team never recovered from the shock; the previous season's stern defence began shipping goals but there was no compensation in attack. Clarke had bought Peter Barnes from West Bromwich for £930,000 but his impact was slight. From December 12 to April 6, in 14 league matches, the team scored just five goals.

His players told themselves they were too good to go down, but the reality was different as Clarke's seemingly authoritative style failed to prevent relegation. He was sacked, yet the fans never turned on him as they had done Jimmy Adamson for he remained a tangible link with fading memories of past glories. Clarke subsequently managed - with mixed success - at Scunthorpe, Barnsley (again) and Lincoln City.

EDDIE GRAY

During long bouts of injury that had denied football his talents, Eddie Gray showed an impressive way when coaching the youngsters at Leeds. With relegation, drastically shrunken gates, high wage bills and the burden of huge transfers fees such as that paid for Peter Barnes, Leeds United, so prosperous under Don Revie, were now impoverished and in debt.

After Allan Clarke, Eddie Gray, who had no managerial experience, was taken on, in the words of one former club executive, as 'a cheap but hopeful option'. He would have to make do with players costing little and any raw talent to hand. If supporters thought the club would, by divine right, return at once to division one, they were to be disappointed. In a somewhat muted 1982/3 season, wherein Leeds drew half their league matches, the club finished ninth.

Matters were not helped by spasms of hooliganism among Leeds fans, the last distraction Eddie Gray wanted. Within his meagre budget, he set about rebuilding the club but, with the notable exception of Andy Ritchie who arrived from Brighton in a swap deal with Terry Connor, Gray's home-grown talent rather than his imports provided Leeds with hope.

Gray's first two seasons saw some dreadfully lukewarm performances by players who seemed to lack the talent and commitment to fulfil Leeds' aspirations. But towards the mid 1980s, things looked promising with the emergence of two brilliant young midfield players John Sheridan and Scott Sellars, the eager, nippy striker Tommy Wright and the composed young Denis Irwin at right back. With Peter Lorimer and Frank Gray having returned as veteran mentors, 1984/5 held the possibility of promotion. But in the end, the team was a mean streak short of dominating the opposition.

Perhaps that realisation troubled the Leeds directors. An uncertain start to Leeds' fourth successive season in the second division was excuse enough for Gray to be sacked along with his assistant Jimmy Lumsden. The players were appalled and supporters demanded his reinstatement. But Gray departed with dignity to be succeeded by Billy Bremner. Meanwhile, the protégés in whom he showed early faith flourished; proof of Gray's vision and a monument to his civilised reign.

MANAGER: JULY 1982 - OCTOBER 1985

BILLY BREMNER

The appointment of Billy Bremner, among the greatest of the Revie old boys, helped dilute the anger generated by Eddie Gray's sacking. Bremner, who had brought both life and promotion to Doncaster Rovers, was a battler and recognised that tough seasoned professionals must be recruited for Leeds to clamber out of division two.

He was to coax some excellent performances from Ian Snodin, one of his own graduates from Doncaster bought by Eddie Gray, and invested in low-budget but eager, reliable players, among them centre-half Jack Ashurst from Carlisle, who exceeded the expectations of many, and Brendan Ormsby from Aston Villa, a brave and vigorous captain.

In 1986/7, things stirred. Bremner produced a tighter, sharper Leeds team that gave little away save in an aberrational 7-2 defeat at Stoke. Sheridan continued to inspire in midfield and Ian Baird, despite his petulance, was a durable and adroit target man. It was, of course, the year an FA Cup Final and promotion double eluded Bremner by a whisker but what really mattered was that the team's exploits restored self-belief and a taste of the big time to Leeds.

Many expected Leeds would have the momentum to make the first division in 1987/8. But despite good signs and good signings such as Peter Haddock and Bobby Davison, there always seemed to be half a dozen more consistent teams in division two. The time for being a team of potential had expired. Leeds directors felt concrete achievements were overdue and a shaky start to 1988/9 saw Bremner among good company when he was sacked from Elland Road in September. Yet there remained a feeling in the air at Elland Road, which Bremner's reign had helped bring about, that good times were not far round the corner.

MANAGER: OCTOBER 1985 - SEPTEMBER 1988

HOWARD WILKINSON

If, by winning the League Championship, Howard Wilkinson has helped expunge Leeds United's obsession with the past, a pining for the distant achievements of the Revie era, it will be the most extraordinary feat of his managerial career. The sense of being champions once more, all the more delicious for its unexpectedness, has the club relishing a future in the big time. While Don Revie had left the club 14 years earlier, until the sacking of Billy Bremner there remained an umbilical cord with Leeds United's godfather. But by 1988, the club had run out of his sons to appoint as manager, and the successes of the past had not drip-fed through them into the present.

Yet it was, in part, the great history created through Revie that made Leeds attractive enough to lure Howard Wilkinson from his first division job at Sheffield Wednesday. There were traditions to live up to but ghosts to be exorcised. A purge of revered old photographs followed the appointment of Wilkinson, by his own admission no more than a journeyman winger with Sheffield Wednesday and Brighton in the 1960s: a less distinguished player than almost all his predecessors. As a manager though with Notts County and Wednesday, he had the knack of winning promotion.

There was no dismemberment of the Bremner side at first though fitness and discipline, for which Wilkinson is renowned, were tightened up. Not until March 1989, near the transfer deadline, did Wilkinson make a startling foray into the transfer market, buying Gordon Strachan, who saw no future as a beleaguered right-winger at Manchester United.

Wilkinson, who has a degree in physical education and is one of football management's most thoughtful pragmatists, had one advantage denied his predecessors. Under the chairmanship of millionaire Leslie Silver, he would not be inhibited from buying whatever players he needed: big ambition needed big financial backing. But an open cheque book can bring headaches, and had Wilkinson made catastrophically expensive mistakes, he would not have been the first manager to do so. As it happened, Strachan, a player of age-defying fitness, proved the most inspirational buy for Leeds since Don Revie bought Bobby Collins.

For 1989/90, to Strachan were added Vinnie Jones, Mel Sterland, John Hendrie, Chris Fairclough and, in mid-season, Lee Chapman: many assertive personalities but none of whom Wilkinson allowed to cause turbulence. There was some but not total emphasis on the long ball game: Leeds had too many good players to jettison all their football instincts. It was a hard, tight promotion race but backed by support as fanatical as at any time in the club's history, Wilkinson led Leeds out of the wilderness and seized the Second Division Championship.

Wilkinson, whose shrewdness and imagination continue to surprise, realised that, with promotion, the club could not stand still. It needed better players. He off-loaded Vinnie Jones, whom he had temporarily tamed and who was a one-season triumph, and brought in Gary McAllister from Leicester, the most accomplished midfielder outside the first division. John Lukic came home from Arsenal to replace Mervyn Day in goal. With Gary Speed and David Batty maturing, Wilkinson was intent on much more than survival. Leeds fans were rewarded with a season of constant excitement, competing on equal terms in epic cup battles against Arsenal and Manchester United, and fourth place in the league, a season almost worthy of the Revie era.

With 1991/2 came even higher ambition: more money lavished on Steve Hodge, Tony Dorigo and Rod Wallace. But throughout, Wilkinson has ensured his regime, his system, contains the players. There are few vapid outbursts from player malcontents in the tabloid press. Leeds United 1991/2 vintage was the best side he had created: mobile, willing, skilful, firm yet lacking in spite - another break with the Revie past. It was a year of constant exposure, a tussle for the First Division Championship almost to the death with the old enemy, Manchester United, that ended in triumph.

In its latter stages, Wilkinson's sensible downbeat approach was crucial in helping players maintain their nerves. It was the Mancunians, the hot favourites, who caved in under the monstrous pressure of fixtures and expectations. Wilkinson, whose mordant post-match remarks about the state of Leeds United and football in general rise to most occasions, could have given his club no more. But, like Revie, he would prefer it if his achievements were less damned with faint praise.

MANAGER: OCTOBER 1988 -

Player	Season	LEAGUE App	Sub	Gls	FA CUP App	Sub	Gls	L CUP App	Sub	Gls	EUROPE App	Sub	Gls	TOTAL App	Sub	Gls
Adams M	86-88	77	(1)	2	6		1	4		0	0		0	87	(1)	3
Addy M	61-62	2		0	0		0	2		0	0		0	4		0
Agana A	1991	1	(1)	0	0		0	0		0	0		0	1	(1)	0
Aizlewood M	86-88	70	(5)	3	1		0	3		0	0		0	74	(5)	3
Andrews I	1988	1		0	0		0	0		0	0		0	1		0
Arins A	1981	0	(1)	0	0		0	0		0	0		0	0	(1)	0
Ashurst J	86-88	93	(1)	1	6		0	6		0	0		0	105	(1)	1
Aspin N	81-88	207	(3)	5	17		0	9		1	0		0	233	(3)	6
Baird I	84-6/87-89	165	(2)	50	8		6	9		1	0		0	182	(2)	57
Balcombe S	1981	1		1	0		0	1		0	0		0	2		1
Barnes P	81-82/83-	56	(2)	5	1		0	5		1	0		0	62	(2)	6
Bates M	66-75	106	(15)	4	10	(4)	1	9	(8)	1	26	(9)	3	151	(36)	9
Batty D	87-	163	(9)	3	9		0	15		0	0		0	187	(9)	3
Beglin J	1989	18	(1)	0	0		0	0		0	0		0	18	(1)	0
Belfitt R	64-71	57	(18)	17	6	(1)	3	17	(2)	5	24	(2)	8	104	(23)	33
Bell W	60-67	204		15	24		1	15		1	17		1	260		18
Blake N	88-89	51		4	2		0	4	(1)	0	0		0	57	(1)	4
Bremner W	59-76	586	(1)	90	69		6	38		3	77		16	770	(1)	115
Brockie V	1987	2		0	0		0	0		0	0		0	2		0
Brown A	82-84	24		1	0		0	0		0	0		0	24		1
Buckley J	86-87	6	(4)	1	0	(1)	0	0		0	0		0	6	(5)	1
Burns K	81-83	54	(2)	2	3		0	7		2	0		0	64	(2)	4
Butterworth A	80-3	54	(10)	15	6		1	4		1	0		0	64	(10)	17
Cameron R	59-61	58		9	2		0	4		2	0		0	64		11
Cantona E	91-	6	(9)	3	0		0	0		0	0		0	6	(9)	3
Carling T	60-61	5		0	0		0	1		0	0		0	6		0
Casey T	1961	3		0	0		0	1		0	0		0	4		0
Caswell B	85-86	9		0	0		0	0		0	0		0	9		0
Chandler J	79-80	21	(5)	2	1		0	1		0	0		0	23	(5)	2
Chapman L	89-	97		49	7		3	12		8	0		0	116		60
Charles J	48-56/62	308		153	19		4	0		0	0		0	327		157
Charlton J	52-72	629		70	52		8	35		7	56		10	772		95
Cherry T	72-82	393	(6)	24	28	(1)	1	35		4	20	(1)	2	476	(8)	31
Clarke A	69-77	270	(3)	110	43	(2)	25	13		2	33		14	359	(5)	151
Collins R	61-66	149		24	13		0	2		1	3		0	167		25
Connor T	79-82	83	(13)	19	6		2	4	(2)	1	0		0	93	(15)	22
Cooper T	63-74	240	(10)	7	30	(1)	0	21		2	48		2	339	(11)	11
Currie A	76-78	102		11	9		0	13		5	0		0	124		16
Curtis A	79-80	28		5	1		0	2		0	4		1	35		6
Davey N	65-71	13	(1)	0	1		0	2		0	4	(2)	0	20	(3)	0
Davison R	87-	79	(11)	31	2	(4)	1	4		1	0		0	85	(15)	33
Day M	84-	225		0	10		0	13		0	0		0	249		0
de Mange K	1987	14	(1)	1	0		0	3		0	0		0	17	(1)	1
Dickinson M	79-85	100	(2)	2	6		0	10		0	0		0	116	(2)	2
Doig R	86-87	3	(3)	0	1		0	1	(2)	0	0		0	5	(5)	0
Donnelly J	82-84	36	(4)	4	1		0	3		0	0		0	40	(4)	4
Dorigo A	91-	38		3	1		0	5		0	0		0	44		3
Edwards K	86-87	29	(14)	8	2	(3)	1	2		0	0		0	33	(17)	9
Edwards M.K	1971	0	(1)	0	0		0	0		0	0		0	0	(1)	0
Eli R	84-85	1	(1)	0	0		0	0		0	0		0	1	(1)	0
Ellam R	72-73	9	(2)	0	2		0	2		0	6		0	19	(2)	0
Entwistle W	1979	7	(4)	2	0	(1)	0	0		0	0		0	7	(5)	2
Fairclough C	88-	127	(1)	14	9		1	12	(1)	0	0		0	136	(3)	16
Faulkner J	69-71	2		0	0		0	0		0	2		0	4		0
Firm N	79-81	11	(1)	0	0		0	0		0	0		0	11	(1)	0
Fitzgerald P	1960	8		0	0		0	0		0	0		0	8		0
Flynn B	77-82	152	(2)	11	6	(1)	0	12		0	4		0	174	(3)	11
Francis G	59-61	46		9	1		0	3		0	0		0	50		9
Galvin C	69-72	6	(1)	1	0	(2)	0	1		0	4	(2)	1	11	5	2
Gavin M	82-84	20	(10)	3	0		0	4	(1)	1	0		0	24	(11)	4
Giles J	63-74	380	(3)	88	61		15	19		1	61	(1)	11	521	4	115
Goodwin F	59-63	107		2	4		0	9		0	0		0	120		2
Graham A	77-82	222	(1)	37	12		3	22		4	3		3	259	(1)	47
Grainger C	1960	33		5	1		0	3		1	0		0	37		6
Gray E	66-84	441	(13)	52	46	(1)	5	33	(2)	6	39	(2)	5	559	(18)	68
Gray F	73-8/81-4	327	(5)	27	27	(1)	3	30	(1)	4	12	(2)	1	396	(9)	35
Grayson S	1987	2		0	0		0	0		0	0		0	2		0
Greenhoff B	79-81	68	(4)	1	1		0	5		0	0		0	74	(4)	1
Greenhoff J	63-68	88	(6)	21	10	(1)	2	12		4	18	(1)	6	128	(8)	33
Haddock P	86-	106	(12)	1	5	(2)	0	9	(2)	0	0		0	120	(16)	1
Hair G	50-63	443		1	21		1	10		0	0		0	474		2
Hallett T	1962	0		0	0		0	1		0	0		0	1		0
Hampton P	71-79	63	(5)	2	5		1	5	(1)	0	3	(1)	0	76	7	
Hamson G	79-85	126	(8)	3	10	(1)	1	4		0	1	(1)	0	141	(10)	4

Dates shown indicate first year of each season. Thus 70-77 means 1970/71 to 1977/78. A single entry indicates one season only, eg 1964 refers to 1964/65.

		LEAGUE			FA CUP			L CUP			EUROPE			TOTAL		
Player	Season	App	Sub	Gls	App	Sub	Gls	App	Sub	Gls	App	Sub	Gls	App	Sub	Gls
Hankin R	76-79	82	(1)	32	1		0	15		3	4		1	102	(1)	36
Harle D	1985	3		0	0		0	0		0	0		0	3		0
Harris C	75-82	123	(30)	26	5		2	7	(7)	1	1	(3)	0	136	(40)	29
Hart P	77-82	191		16	11		1	17		1	4		2	223		20
Harvey D	65-79/82-4	350		0	31		0	38		0	25	(2)	0	444	(2)	0
Hawkins D	65-67	2		0	0		0	2		0	0		0	4		0
Hawksby J	60-63	37		2	1		0	7		0	0		0	45		2
Hawley J	78-79	30	(3)	16	3		0	6		1	0		0	39	(3)	17
Henderson T	62-64	24		2	6		0	4		0	0		0	34		2
Hendrie J	1989	22	(5)	5	1		0	1		0	0		0	24	(5)	5
Hibbitt T	66-70	32	(15)	9	1		0	5		0	8	(2)	2	46	(17)	11
Hilaire V	88-89	42	(3)	6	2		0	3		1	0		0	47	(3)	7
Hird K	78-83	165	(16)	19	6	(2)	2	7	(1)	0	3		0	181	(19)	21
Hodge S	91-	12	(12)	7	1		0	3	(1)	0	0		0	16	(13)	7
Hughes P	83-84	6		0	1			0		0	0		0	7		0
Humphreys A	59-61	40		0	1		0	3		0	0		0	44		0
Hunter N	62-76	540		18	65	(1)	1	39		1	78	(1)	1	722	(2)	21
Irwin D	83-85	72		1	3		0	5		0	0		0	80		1
Johanneson A	60-69	167	(2)	48	14		5	8		6	5	(1)	8	194	(3)	67
Johnson R	62-67	18	(4)	4	1		1	6	(1)	1	0		0	25	(5)	6
Jones A	60-61	25		0	1		0	3		0	0		0	29		0
Jones M	67-73	216	(4)	77	36		12	13	(1)	5	42		17	307	(5)	111
Jones V	1989	43	(2)	5	1		0	2		0	0		0	46	(2)	5
Jordan J	71-77	139	(30)	35	16	(3)	4	9	(1)	3	18	(4)	6	182	38	48
Kamara C	89-91	15	(5)	1	0		0	1	(2)	0	0		0	16	(7)	1
Kelly G	1991-	0	(2)	0	0		0	0	(1)	0	0		0	0	(3)	0
Kennedy D	69-70	2		1	0		0	0		0	1		0	3		1
Kerr D	88 -	3	(5)	0	1		0	0		0	0		0	4	(5)	0
Kilford J	58-61	21		0	0		0	2		0	0		0	23		0
Lawson I	61-64	44		17	3		1	4		3	0		0	51		21
Letheran G	73-74	1		0	0		0	0		0	0	(1)	0	1	(1)	0
Liddell G	72-74	2	(1)	0	0		0	1		0	1	(1)	1	4	(2)	1
Linighan A	84-85	66		3	2		0	6		1	0		0	74		4
Lorimer P	62-78/83-5	503	(22)	168	56	(3)	20	41	(1)	19	74	(1)	30	674	(27)	237
Lukic J	78-82/90	227		0	15		0	18		0	3		0	263		0
Lumsden J	66-69	3	(1)	0	0		0	0		0	0		0	3	(1)	0
McAdams W	1961	11		3	2		1	0		0	0		0	13		4
McAllister G	1990-	79	(1)	7	7		1	11		2	0		0	97	(1)	10
McClelland J	1989-92	22	(2)	0	2		0	2	(1)	0	0		0	26	(3)	0
McCluskey G	83-85	57	(6)	16	4		0	5	(3)	1	0		0	66	(9)	17
McCole J	59-61	78		45	2		1	5		7	0		0	85		53
McConnell P	58-61	48		4	2		0	3		1	0		0	53		5
McDonald R	86-87	23		1	0		0	1		0	0		0	24		1
McGhie W	1976	2		1	0		0	0		0	0		0	2		1
McGinley W	72-73	0	(1)	0	0		0	0		0	0	(1)	0	0	(2)	0
McGoldrick J	1983	7		0	3		0	2		0	0		0	12		0
McGovern J	1974	4		0	0		0	0		0	0		0	4		0
McGregor J	1985	5		0	0		0	0		0	0		0	5		0
McKenzie D	74-75	64	(2)	27	6	(3)	2	5		1	1		0	76	(5)	30
McNab N	1982	5		0	1		0	0		0	0		0	6		0
McNiven J	75-77	15	(7)	6	0		0	1		0	0		0	16	(7)	6
McQueen G	72-77	140		15	13		1	5		0	12	(1)	3	170	(1)	19
Madeley P	64-79	528	(8)	25	64	(3)	2	49	(1)	3	70	(1)	4	711	(13)	34
Maguire P	1987	2		0	0		0	0		0	0		0	2		0
Mann J	71-73	2		0	0		0	0	(1)	0	2		0	4	(1)	0
Mason C	61-62	31		0	0		0	2		0	0		0	33		0
Mayers D	1961	20		5	2		0	2		0	0		0	24		5
Melrose J	1987	3	(1)	0	0	(1)	0	0	(1)	0	0		0	3	(3)	0
Mumby P	87-88	3	(3)	0	0		0	0	(2)	1	0		0	3	(5)	1
Newsome J	91 -	6	(3)	2	0		0	0		0	0		0	6	(3)	2
Noteman K	1987	0	(1)	0	0		0	0		0	0		0	0	(1)	0
O'Donnell C	1989	0	(1)	0	0		0	0		0	0		0	0	(1)	0
O'Grady M	65-69	90	(1)	12	5		1	5		0	20		3	120	(1)	16
O'Hare J	1974	6		1	0		0	1		0	0		0	7		1
O'Neill J	1973	0	(1)	0	0		0	0		0	0	(2)	0	0	(3)	0
Ormsby B	85-88	51		6	4		1	1		0	0		0	56		7
Parker N	1977	0	(1)	0	0		0	0		0	0		0	0	(1)	0
Parkinson K	75-80	25	(6)	0	1		0	4		0	2		0	32	(6)	0
Parlane D	79-82	45	(5)	10	2		0	1		0	0		0	48	(5)	10
Peacock A	63-66	54		27	6		2	2		1	3		1	65		31
Pearson J	86-90	55	(48)	12	5	(4)	0	5	(4)	0	0		0	65	(56)	12
Peterson P	1969	3	(1)	0	0		0	0		0	0		0	3	(1)	0
Peyton N	58-62	105		17	3		1	9		2	0		0	117		20
Phelan T	1985	12	(2)	0	0		0	3		0	0		0	15	(2)	0
Reaney P	62-77	549	(8)	6	72	(1)	3	39		0	74	(3)	0	734	(12)	9
Rennie D	85-88	95	(6)	5	7		1	7		0	0		0	109	(6)	6
Revie D	58-61	76		11	1		0	3		1	0		0	80		12
Ritchie A	82-86	129	(10)	40	9		1	11		3	0		0	149	(10)	44
Robinson R	85-86	27		0	0		0	0		0	0		0	27		0

Dates shown indicate first year of each season. Thus 70-77 means 1970/71 to 1977/78. A single entry indicates one season only, eg 1964 refers to 1964/65.

Player	Season	LEAGUE			FA CUP			L CUP			EUROPE			TOTAL		
		App	Sub	Gls	App	Sub	Gls	App	Sub	Gls	App	Sub	Gls	App	Sub	Gls
Sabella A	1980	22	(1)	2	2		0	2		0	0		0	26	(1)	2
Sellars S	82-85	72	(4)	12	4		0	4	1		0		0	80	(4)	13
Shaw J	71-73	0		0	0		0	0		0	2		0	2		0
Sheridan J	82-88	230	(5)	48	11	(1)	1	14		3	0		0	255	(6)	52
Shutt C	88-	40	(30)	18	6		0	5	(2)	1	0		0	51	(32)	19
Sibbald R	66-67	1	(1)	0	0		0	0		0	0		0	1	(1)	0
Simmonds L	84-85	6	(3)	3	0		0	0		0	0		0	6	(3)	3
Sinclair R	1986	8		0	0		0	1		0	0		0	9		0
Smith E	60-62	65		3	3		0	3		0	0		0	71		3
Snodin G	87-90	86	(11)	10	5	(2)	0	5	(1)	2	0		0	96	(14)	12
Snodin I	85-86	51		6	1		0	3		2	0		0	55		8
Speed G	88-	89	(15)	17	7	(1)	0	11		6	0		0	107	(16)	23
Sprake G	61-72	380		0	45		0	22		0	57	(2)	0	504	(2)	0
Sterland M	89-	108	(2)	16	8		1	13		1	0		0	129	(2)	18
Stevenson B	74-81	88	(7)	4	5		0	7	(1)	1	2		0	102	(8)	5
Stewart D	73-78	55		0	8		0	6		0	5		0	74		0
Stiles J	84-88	51	(15)	2	5		1	4	(2)	0	0		0	60	(17)	3
Storrie J	62-66	123	(3)	58	12		3	8		5	10		1	153	(3)	67
Strachan G	88-	126	(1)	30	7		1	13		1	0		0	146	(1)	32
Swan P	85-88	43	(6)	11	3		0	3		2	0		0	49	(6)	13
Swinburne T	1985	2		0	0		0	0		0	0		0	2		0
Taylor R	85-88	33	(9)	9	1		0	5	(1)	3	0		0	39	(10)	12
Thomas G	74-83	79	(10)	3	4	(1)	0	9		0	0		0	92	(11)	3
Thomas M	1989	3		0	0		0	0		0	0		0	3		0
Thompson N	83-86	6	(1)	0	2		0	0		0	0		0	8	(1)	0
Turner C	1989	2		0	0		0	0		0	0		0	2		0
Varadi I	89-	19	(3)	4	0		0	1		0	0		0	20	(3)	4
Wallace Rod	91-	34		11	1		0	3		2	0		0	38		13
Watson A	83-84	37	(1)	7	1		0	4		0	0		0	42	(1)	7
Weston D	62-64	68		24	7		1	3		1	0		0	78		26
Wetherall D	91-	0	(1)	0	0		0	0		0	0		0	0	(1)	0
Whitlow M	88-91	62	(15)	4	1	(4)	0	3	(1)	0	0		0	66	(20)	4
Whyte C	90-	79		4	5		0	12		1	0		0	96		5
Whyte D	1976	1	(1)	0	0		0	0		0	0		0	1	(1)	0
Williams A	88-91	25	(22)	3	2		0	3	(3)	0	0		0	30	(25)	3
Williams G	87-88	39		3	1	(1)	0	4		0	0		0	44	(1)	3
Williamson B	63-65	5		0	1		0	2		0	0		0	8		0
Worthington F	81-2	32		14	0		0	3		1	0		0	35		15
Wright B	62-65	5		0	0		0	3		0	0		0	8		0
Wright T	82-85	73	(8)	24	4		3	3	(3)	1	0		0	80	(11)	28
Yorath T	67-76	121	(21)	10	14	(3)	1	10	(1)	0	20	(7)	1	165	(32)	12
Younger T	61-62	37		0	2		0	3		0	0		0	42		0

Dates shown indicate first year of each season. Thus 70-77 means 1970/71 to 1977/78. A single entry indicates one season only, eg 1964 refers to 1964/65.

LEEDS UNITED FACTS AND FIGURES

ADDRESS: Elland Road, Leeds, LS11 0ES.

Founded 1904 as Leeds City. Expelled from the league and wound up by the FA in October 1919 after allegations of illegal payments to players. The reformed club, Leeds United, was elected to the Football League on May 31 1920.

HONOURS.
European Cup runners-up: 1974/5. European Cup-Winners' Cup runners-up: 1972/3.
Inter Cities Fairs Cup winners: 1967/8, 1970/1. Runners-up 1966/7.
Division One Champions: 1968/9, 1970/1, 1991/2. Runners-up: 1964/5, 1965/6, 1969/70, 1970/1, 1971/2.
Division Two Champions: 1923/4, 1963/4, 1989/90.
Division Two Runners-Up: 1927/8, 1931/2, 1955/6.
FA Cup Winners: 1971-2. FA Cup Finalists: 1964/5, 1969/70, 1972/3.
League Cup Winners: 1967/8.
Most League Appearances: Jack Charlton: 629 (1952/72).
Most League Goals: Peter Lorimer: 168 (1962/78, 1983/5).
Most Capped Player: Billy Bremner, 54, Scotland. (1965-76).